favourite
family meals

First published in 2010
LOVE FOOD is an imprint of Parragon Books Ltd

Parragon
Queen Street House
4 Queen Street
Bath BA1 1HE, UK

ISBN: 978-1-4075-4764-0

Printed in China

Cover design by Andrew Easton at Ummagumma
Internal design concept by Fiona Roberts
Recipes and photography by the Bridgewater Book Company Ltd

Notes for the Reader

This book uses both metric and imperial measurements. Follow the same units of measurement throughout; do not mix metric and imperial. All spoon measurements are level: teaspoons are assumed to be 5 ml, and tablespoons are assumed to be 15 ml. Unless otherwise stated, milk is assumed to be full fat, eggs and individual vegetables are medium, and pepper is freshly ground black pepper.

The times given are an approximate guide only. Preparation times differ according to the techniques used by different people and the cooking times may also vary from those given. Optional ingredients, variations or serving suggestions have not been included in the calculations.

Recipes using raw or very lightly cooked eggs should be avoided by infants, the elderly, pregnant women, convalescents and anyone suffering from an illness. Pregnant and breastfeeding women are advised to avoid eating peanuts and peanut products. Sufferers from nut allergies should be aware that some of the ready-made ingredients used in the recipes in this book may contain nuts. Always check the packaging before use.

Vegetarians should be aware that some of the ready-made ingredients used in the recipes in this book may contain animal products. Always check the packaging before use.

favourite
family meals

over 100 recipes to enjoy

contents

contents

Roasting

Cookies & Bars

Introduction

Preparing nutritious, healthy and tasty meals is one of the most important aspects of raising a happy, fit and contented family. Most of us have a repertoire of favourite dishes that make a regular appearance at the dinner table but sometimes our creativity fails us and even the keenest cooks can run out of ideas. Variety is said to be the spice of life and it is certainly the key to a well-balanced diet and to making family meals interesting and enjoyable occasions. *Family Meals* provides the family cook with the answers to those never-ending questions: what would be quick and easy for a midweek supper, what shall I cook for dinner on Saturday, what would make a nice change for Sunday lunch...? Furthermore, it answers these questions in a variety of helpful ways.

The book is divided into four sections and each section contains several chapters offering an at-a-glance choice of delicious dishes using your favourite ingredients. If you want something hearty and warming, for example, turn to the section on Stews & Casseroles and then select the type that appeals — meat, poultry and game, seafood or vegetable — and browse through the relevant chapter until you find exactly the dish to fit the bill. Perhaps you want to encourage the family to eat more fish — always a healthy option — and need to find

ENTICING RECIPE. TRY THE CHAPTER ON FISH IN THE SECTION ON ROASTING FOR A TEMPTINGLY DIFFERENT DISH. EQUALLY, YOU MIGHT HAVE SOME FRESH VEGETABLES IN THE REFRIGERATOR AND PASTA IN THE STORECUPBOARD BUT NEED A BIT OF INSPIRATION ABOUT HOW TO COMBINE THEM INTO AN APPEALING SUPPER.

THERE ARE WELL OVER 100 RECIPES, MANY OF THEM IDEAL FOR MIDWEEK MEALS WHEN TIME IS LIMITED. OTHERS ARE THE PERFECT CHOICE FOR MORE LEISURELY COOKING AT THE WEEKEND. EITHER WAY, THEY ARE ALL EASY TO FOLLOW WHETHER YOU'RE A BEGINNER OR AN EXPERIENCED COOK. THE RANGE OF INGREDIENTS IS VAST AND ALTHOUGH THERE ARE SOME RATHER MORE SPECIAL DISHES AS WELL AS MANY ECONOMICAL MEALS, THEY ARE ALL VALUE-FOR-MONEY WITH NOTHING EXTRAVAGANT OR DIFFICULT TO FIND.

THERE ARE LOTS OF DISHES FROM AROUND THE WORLD, SO YOU ARE SURE TO FIND PLENTY THAT YOU CAN GUARANTEE WILL WHET YOUR FAMILY'S APPETITE WHATEVER THEIR FAVOURITE FLAVOURS. THERE ARE TRIED AND TESTED CLASSICS THAT ARE ALWAYS A SURE-FIRE SUCCESS AND SOME MORE UNUSUAL, PERHAPS UNFAMILIAR, RECIPES THAT WILL BE FUN AND INTRIGUING BOTH TO COOK AND TASTE. THERE ARE EVEN SCRUMPTIOUS COOKIES AND BARS THAT ARE GREAT ON THEIR OWN, DELICIOUS WITH ICE CREAM OR YOGURT FOR DESSERT AND POPULAR ADDITIONS TO PACKED LUNCHES.

There is surely no other food that could be simpler. Pasta, the national dish of Italy yet eaten all over the world, is made from just durum wheat flour and water, and sometimes enriched with egg or oil. But though it may be the simplest food, it is probably the most varied.

It comes in over 650 different shapes and sizes, and can be flavoured with herbs, spinach or tomato. To add to the confusion, names can vary from one manufacturer to another and, in Italy, vary from region to region, so what might be fettuccine in one region might be pappardelle in another!

Basic recipes

Basic Pasta Dough

This is the most basic recipe for making pasta dough by hand or using a food processor. You can add colourings and flavourings according to the dish (see right).

sift the flour into the bowl of the food processor and add the salt. Pour in the eggs and olive oil, add any flavouring, and process until the dough begins to come together.

Turn out the dough on to a lightly floured work surface and knead until smooth. Wrap the dough in clingfilm and leave to rest for at least 30 minutes before rolling out or feeding through a pasta machine, as this makes it more elastic. Use as required.

Flavoured Pasta

tomato pasta: Add 2 tablespoons tomato purée to the flour when making the dough and use 1½ eggs instead of 2.
herb pasta: Add 3 tablespoons chopped fresh herbs to the flour.
spinach pasta: Squeeze out as much liquid as possible from 150 g/5½ oz thawed frozen spinach or 225 g/8 oz fresh spinach blanched in boiling water for 1 minute. Chop finely and mix thoroughly with the flour.
wholemeal pasta: Use 140 g/5 oz wholemeal flour sifted with 25 g/1 oz plain white flour.

Béchamel Sauce

MAKES 300 ml/10 fl oz

INTRODUCTION TO
PASTA

SERVES 3–4
200 g/7 oz plain white flour or strong white
  bread flour, plus extra for dusting
pinch of salt
2 eggs, lightly beaten
1 tbsp olive oil
To make the pasta dough by hand, sift the flour and salt on to a clean work surface and make a well in the centre. Pour the eggs and oil into the well, then using your fingers, gradually combine the eggs and oil and incorporate the flour. Turn out the dough on to a lightly floured work surface and knead until smooth. Wrap the dough in clingfilm and leave to rest for at least 30 minutes before rolling out or feeding through a pasta machine, as this makes it more elastic. Use as required.
Alternatively, if you wish to use a food processor,

300 ml/10 fl oz milk
1 bay leaf
6 black peppercorns
slice of onion
mace blade
25 g/1 oz butter
25 g/1 oz plain flour
salt and pepper
Pour the milk into a saucepan and add the bay leaf, peppercorns, onion and mace. Heat gently to just below boiling point, then remove from the heat, cover and leave to infuse for 10 minutes. Sieve the milk into a jug.
Melt the butter in a separate saucepan. Sprinkle in the flour and cook over a low heat, stirring constantly, for 1 minute. Remove from the heat and gradually stir in the milk. Return to the heat and bring to the boil, stirring. Cook, stirring, until thickened and smooth. Season to taste with salt and pepper.

With such a variety available, pasta is a very versatile food which can be served hot or cold in many dishes, including not only main meals but soups, starters and light meals as the recipes in this chapter illustrate.

Some types of pasta are specially designed for soups as they cook in a short time. These include small rings of anellini, small shells of conchigliette, small butterflies of farfalline and stars of stelline, along with many more. For children there are small shapes of the alphabet, known as alfabeto, which are always popular. Pasta soups are ideal for using up all those odds and ends of pasta that you have tucked away in the storecupboard, as in the recipe for White Bean Soup. Get them out now and use them up!

In Italy, pasta is served as a first course, and although this may seem rather substantial to those not used to it, it is because servings

LIGHT DISHES

are small and may be followed by a simple grilled fish or meat dish, without numerous accompaniments. Pasta also makes an ideal salad base for a perfect light lunch or supper dish. What could be more tempting on a summer's day than a Mediterranean-style salad of griddled fresh tuna steaks, spirals of pasta, green beans and tomatoes, tossed in a lemony dressing, or pasta shells and chargrilled peppers tossed in pesto? It makes your mouth water just thinking about it!

SERVES 6

2 tbsp olive oil

55 g/2 oz rindless pancetta or streaky
    bacon, diced

2 onions, sliced

2 garlic cloves, finely chopped

3 carrots, chopped

2 celery sticks, chopped

225 g/8 oz dried haricot beans,

soaked in cold water to cover
    for 3–4 hours

400 g/14 oz canned chopped
    tomatoes

2 litres/3½ pints beef stock

350 g/12 oz potatoes, diced

175 g/6 oz dried pepe bucato,
    macaroni or other soup
    pasta shapes

175 g/6 oz French beans, sliced

115 g/4 oz fresh or frozen peas

225 g/8 oz Savoy cabbage, shredded

3 tbsp chopped fresh flat-leaf parsley

salt and pepper

fresh Parmesan cheese shavings,
    to serve

Minestrone Milanese

It usually takes 1–1½ hours of cooking for soaked haricot beans to become tender, but this can vary depending on how long they have been stored.

• Heat the olive oil in a large, heavy-based saucepan. Add the pancetta, onions and garlic and cook, stirring occasionally, for 5 minutes.

• Add the carrots and celery and cook, stirring occasionally, for a further 5 minutes, or until all the vegetables are softened.

• Drain the haricot beans and add them to the saucepan with the tomatoes and their can juices and the beef stock. Bring to the boil, reduce the heat, cover and leave to simmer for 1 hour.

• Add the potatoes, re-cover and cook for 15 minutes, then add the pasta, French beans, peas, cabbage and parsley. Cover and cook for a further 15 minutes, or until all the vegetables are tender. Season to taste with salt and pepper. Ladle into warmed soup bowls and serve immediately with Parmesan cheese shavings.

SERVES 4

175 g/6 oz dried cannellini beans, soaked overnight in cold water to cover

1.7 litres/3 pints chicken or vegetable stock

115 g/4 oz dried corallini, conchigliette piccole or other soup pasta

6 tbsp olive oil

2 garlic cloves, finely chopped

4 tbsp chopped fresh flat-leaf parsley

salt and pepper

fresh crusty bread, to serve

White Bean Soup

Beans feature widely in Tuscan cuisine. This smooth, comforting soup, in which beans are simmered for 2 hours, is very simple to make. Garlic and parsley, stirred in just before serving, complement the flavour, and a drizzle of olive oil adds the final touch.

• Drain the soaked beans and place them in a large, heavy-based saucepan. Add the stock and bring to the boil. Partially cover the saucepan, reduce the heat and leave to simmer for 2 hours, or until tender.

• Transfer about half the beans and a little of the stock to a food processor or blender and process to a smooth purée. Return the purée to the saucepan and stir well to mix. Return the soup to the boil.

• Add the pasta to the soup, return to the boil and cook for 10 minutes, or until tender.

• Meanwhile, heat 4 tablespoons of the olive oil in a small saucepan. Add the garlic and cook over a low heat, stirring frequently, for 4–5 minutes, or until golden. Stir the garlic into the soup and add the parsley. Season to taste with salt and pepper and ladle into warmed soup bowls. Drizzle with the remaining olive oil and serve immediately with crusty bread.

SERVES 4

350 g/12 oz dried ziti, broken into
    4-cm/1½-inch lengths

5 tbsp extra virgin olive oil

2 garlic cloves, lightly crushed

200 g/7 oz rocket

2 fresh red chillies, thickly sliced

salt

fresh red chilli flowers, to garnish

freshly grated pecorino cheese,
    to serve

Ziti with Rocket

Wild rocket has a more pungent, peppery flavour than the cultivated variety. However, if you find it is too strong, blanch the leaves for 1 minute in boiling water and pat dry before stir-frying.

• Bring a large, heavy-based saucepan of lightly salted water to the boil. Add the pasta, return to the boil and cook for 8–10 minutes, or until tender but still firm to the bite.

• Meanwhile, heat the olive oil in a large, heavy-based frying pan. Add the garlic, rocket and chillies and stir-fry for 5 minutes, or until the rocket has wilted.

• Stir 2 tablespoons of the pasta cooking water into the rocket, then drain the pasta and add to the frying pan. Cook, stirring frequently, for 2 minutes, then transfer to a warmed serving dish. Remove and discard the garlic cloves and chillies, garnish with red chilli flowers and serve immediately with the pecorino cheese.

SERVES 4

450 g/1 lb dried farfalle

25 g/1 oz unsalted butter

350 g/12 oz petits pois

200 ml/7 fl oz double cream

pinch of freshly grated nutmeg

salt and pepper

fresh flat-leaf parsley sprigs,
    to garnish

55 g/2 oz freshly grated Parmesan
    cheese, plus extra to serve

crusty bread, to serve

Farfalle with Cream & Parmesan

This dish is traditionally named fettucine Alfredo and is made without the petits pois. Adding the petits pois creates a more substantial meal.

• Bring a large saucepan of lightly salted water to the boil. Add the pasta, return to the boil and cook for 8–10 minutes, or until tender but still firm to the bite, then drain thoroughly.

• Melt the butter in a large, heavy-based saucepan. Add the petits pois and cook for 2–3 minutes. Add 150 ml/5 fl oz of the cream and bring to the boil. Reduce the heat and simmer for 1 minute, or until slightly thickened.

• Add the drained pasta to the cream mixture. Place the saucepan over a low heat and toss until the farfalle are thoroughly coated. Season to taste with nutmeg, salt and pepper, then add the remaining cream and the grated Parmesan cheese. Toss again and transfer to individual serving bowls. Garnish with parsley sprigs and serve immediately with extra Parmesan cheese for sprinkling and crusty bread.

SERVES 4

2 tbsp lemon juice

4 baby globe artichokes

7 tbsp olive oil

2 shallots, finely chopped

2 garlic cloves, finely chopped

2 tbsp chopped fresh flat-leaf parsley

2 tbsp chopped fresh mint

350 g/12 oz dried rigatoni or other
     tubular pasta

12 large raw prawns

25 g/1 oz unsalted butter

salt and pepper

Springtime Pasta

Large Mediterranean prawns, known as gamberoni in Italy, have a superb flavour and a texture which is superior to that of the very big tiger prawns, but they may be difficult to obtain.

• Fill a large bowl with cold water and add the lemon juice. Prepare the artichokes one at a time. Cut off the stems and trim away any tough outer leaves. Cut across the tops of the leaves. Slice in half lengthways and remove the central fibrous chokes, then cut lengthways into 5-mm/¼-inch thick slices. Immediately place the slices in the bowl of acidulated water to prevent discoloration.

• Heat 5 tablespoons of the olive oil in a heavy-based frying pan. Drain the artichoke slices and pat dry with kitchen paper. Add them to the frying pan with the shallots, garlic, parsley and mint and cook over a low heat, stirring frequently, for 10–12 minutes, or until tender.

• Meanwhile, bring a large saucepan of lightly salted water to the boil. Add the pasta, return to the boil and cook for 8–10 minutes, or until tender but still firm to the bite.

• Peel the prawns, cut a slit along the back of each and remove and discard the dark vein. Melt the butter in a small frying pan, cut the prawns in half and add them to the frying pan. Cook, stirring occasionally, for 2–3 minutes, or until they have changed colour. Season to taste with salt and pepper.

• Drain the pasta and tip it into a bowl. Add the remaining olive oil and toss well. Add the artichoke mixture and the prawns and toss again. Serve immediately.

SERVES 4

350 g/12 oz dried bavettine

2 tbsp olive oil

1 garlic clove, finely chopped

115 g/4 oz smoked salmon, cut into
   thin strips

55 g/2 oz rocket

salt and pepper

½ lemon, to garnish

Bavettine with Smoked Salmon & Rocket

Do not overcook the salmon or rocket; they should just be warmed through and the rocket lightly wilted. If rocket is unavailable, use baby spinach leaves instead.

- Bring a large, heavy-based saucepan of lightly salted water to the boil. Add the pasta, return to the boil and cook for 8–10 minutes, or until tender but still firm to the bite.
- Just before the end of the cooking time, heat the olive oil in a heavy-based frying pan. Add the garlic and cook over a low heat, stirring constantly, for 1 minute. Do not allow the garlic to brown or it will taste bitter. Add the salmon and rocket. Season to taste with salt and pepper and cook, stirring constantly, for 1 minute. Remove the frying pan from the heat.
- Drain the pasta and transfer to a warmed serving dish. Add the smoked salmon and rocket mixture, toss lightly and serve, garnished with a lemon half.

SERVES 4

115 g/4 oz French beans, cut into
5-cm/2-inch lengths

225 g/8 oz dried fusilli tricolore

100 ml/3½ fl oz olive oil

2 tuna steaks, about 350 g/12 oz each

6 cherry tomatoes, halved

55 g/2 oz black olives, stoned and
halved

6 canned anchovies, drained and
chopped

3 tbsp chopped fresh flat-leaf parsley

2 tbsp lemon juice

8–10 radicchio leaves

salt and pepper

Pasta Niçoise

Brushing or spraying the griddle pan with oil helps prevent the food sticking. After cooking, leave the griddle pan to cool. Do not plunge it into cold water as this may warp the pan.

• Bring a large, heavy-based saucepan of lightly salted water to the boil. Add the French beans, reduce the heat and cook for 5–6 minutes. Remove with a slotted spoon and refresh in a bowl of cold water. Drain well. Add the pasta to the same saucepan, return to the boil and cook for 8–10 minutes, or until tender but still firm to the bite.

• Meanwhile, brush a griddle pan with some of the olive oil and heat until smoking. Season the tuna to taste with salt and pepper and brush both sides with some of the remaining olive oil. Cook over a medium heat for 2 minutes on each side, or until cooked to your liking, then remove from the griddle pan and reserve.

• Drain the pasta well and tip it into a bowl. Add the French beans, cherry tomatoes, olives, anchovies, parsley, lemon juice and remaining olive oil and season to taste with salt and pepper. Toss well and leave to cool. Remove and discard any skin from the tuna and slice thickly.

• Gently mix the tuna into the pasta salad. Line a large salad bowl with the radicchio leaves, spoon in the salad and serve.

SERVES 4

1 red pepper

1 orange pepper

280 g/10 oz dried conchiglie

5 tbsp extra virgin olive oil

2 tbsp lemon juice

2 tbsp green pesto

1 garlic clove, finely chopped

3 tbsp shredded fresh basil leaves

salt and pepper

Pasta Salad with Chargrilled Peppers

A more traditional salad, without the pasta, can be made in the same way. When the peppers have been under the grill for 10 minutes, add 4 tomatoes and grill for a further 5 minutes, then remove from the grill. Cover the peppers with kitchen paper, then peel and chop as above. Peel and roughly chop the tomatoes. Combine them with the pesto dressing and garnish with black olives.

• Preheat the grill. Put the whole peppers on a baking sheet and place under the hot grill, turning frequently, for 15 minutes, or until charred all over. Remove with tongs and place in a bowl. Cover with crumpled kitchen paper and reserve.

• Meanwhile, bring a large saucepan of lightly salted water to the boil. Add the pasta, return to the boil and cook for 8–10 minutes, or until tender but still firm to the bite.

• Combine the olive oil, lemon juice, pesto and garlic in a bowl, whisking well to mix. Drain the pasta, add it to the pesto mixture while still hot and toss well. Reserve until required.

• When the peppers are cool enough to handle, peel off the skins, then cut open and remove the seeds. Chop the flesh roughly and add to the pasta with the basil. Season to taste with salt and pepper and toss well. Serve.

SERVES 4

225 g/8 oz dried farfalle or other pasta
    shapes
6 pieces of sun-dried tomato in oil,
    drained and chopped
4 spring onions, chopped
55 g/2 oz rocket, shredded
½ cucumber, deseeded and diced

2 tbsp freshly grated Parmesan
    cheese
salt and pepper

DRESSING
4 tbsp olive oil
½ tsp caster sugar
1 tbsp white wine vinegar

1 tsp Dijon mustard
4 fresh basil leaves, finely shredded
salt and pepper

Warm Pasta Salad

It makes it easier to toss the pasta if you use 2 forks or 2 dessertspoons. Before adding the dressing to the salad, whisk it again until emulsified. Add just before serving.

• To make the dressing, whisk the olive oil, sugar, vinegar and mustard together in a jug. Season to taste with salt and pepper and stir in the basil.

• Bring a large, heavy-based saucepan of lightly salted water to the boil. Add the pasta, return to the boil and cook for 8–10 minutes, or until tender but still firm to the bite. Drain and transfer to a salad bowl. Add the dressing and toss well.

• Add the chopped sun-dried tomatoes, spring onions, rocket and cucumber, season to taste with salt and pepper and toss. Sprinkle with the Parmesan cheese and serve warm.

Of all the pasta dishes in the world, Bolognese meat sauce (ragù), served with spaghetti, is probably the best loved. However, Spaghetti Bolognese isn't Italian at all but a British invention. In Italy they would never serve so much sauce with their pasta. The sauce would be cooked slowly for several hours, and Italians traditionally eat Bolognese sauce with tagliatelle, not spaghetti! When it comes to choosing a variety of pasta to serve with a particular sauce, suggestions are given in the recipes but, should you wish to use another shape, although there are no hard and fast rules, there is a general rule of thumb. Long, thin pasta are ideal for simple sauces such as Pesto, while thicker strands are good with a meat, fish, cheese, cream, mushroom or smooth tomato sauce. Short, tubular pasta, twists and shells, which have hollows and cavities for the sauce to cling to, go well with thicker, chunkier sauces.

SIMPLE SAUCES

There is a vast choice of sauces to dress pasta, from the simplest Pesto to Pumpkin or Chicken & Porcini. What is important is that the pasta isn't drowned in the sauce. There should be just enough sauce to coat it lightly and not leave a pool on the plate once the pasta has been eaten. Finally, don't overlook the quickest pasta sauce that you can make – melted butter or olive oil with plenty of freshly ground black pepper and perhaps a handful of chopped fresh herbs. It is often the simple things in life that are the best!

SERVES 4

2 tbsp olive oil

1 tbsp butter

1 small onion, finely chopped

1 carrot, finely chopped

1 celery stick, finely chopped

50 g/1¾ oz mushrooms, diced

225 g/8 oz fresh beef mince

75 g/2¾ oz unsmoked bacon or ham, diced

2 chicken livers, chopped

2 tbsp tomato purée

125 ml/4 fl oz dry white wine

½ tsp freshly grated nutmeg

300 ml/10 fl oz chicken stock

125 ml/4 fl oz double cream

450 g/1 lb dried spaghetti

salt and pepper

2 tbsp chopped fresh flat-leaf parsley, to garnish

freshly grated Parmesan, to serve

Spaghetti Bolognese

This classic meat sauce (ragù) from Bologna can also be made with minced veal or half beef and half pork, and the cream can be omitted. If you choose to omit it, and the sauce becomes too dry, add a little warm water.

- Heat the olive oil and butter in a large saucepan over a medium heat. Add the onion, carrot, celery and mushrooms to the saucepan, then fry until soft. Add the beef and bacon and fry until the beef is evenly browned.
- Stir in the chicken livers and tomato purée and cook for 2–3 minutes. Pour in the wine and season with salt, pepper and the nutmeg. Add the stock. Bring to the boil, then cover and simmer gently over a low heat for 1 hour. Stir in the cream and simmer, uncovered, until reduced.
- Bring a large saucepan of lightly salted water to the boil. Add the pasta, return to the boil and cook until tender but still firm to the bite. Drain and transfer to a warmed serving dish.
- Spoon the meat sauce over the pasta, garnish with parsley and serve with Parmesan cheese.

SERVES 4

3 tbsp olive oil

1 onion, chopped

1 red pepper, deseeded and diced

1 orange pepper, deseeded and diced

800 g/1 lb 12 oz canned chopped
  tomatoes

1 tbsp sun-dried tomato paste

1 tsp paprika

225 g/8 oz pepperoni sausage, sliced

2 tbsp chopped fresh flat-leaf parsley,
  plus extra to garnish

450 g/1 lb dried garganelli

salt and pepper

mixed salad leaves, to serve

Pepperoni Pasta

Pepperoni is a hotly spiced Italian sausage made from pork and beef and flavoured with fennel. You could substitute other spicy sausages, such as kabanos or chorizo, if you like. If you cannot find garganelli pasta, then use penne or another pasta shape, such as fusilli, bucati or farfalle.

• Heat 2 tablespoons of the olive oil in a large, heavy-based frying pan. Add the onion and cook over a low heat, stirring occasionally, for 5 minutes, or until softened. Add the red and orange peppers, tomatoes and their can juices, sun-dried tomato paste and paprika and bring to the boil.

• Add the pepperoni and parsley and season to taste with salt and pepper. Stir well, bring to the boil, then reduce the heat and simmer for 10–15 minutes.

• Meanwhile, bring a large, heavy-based saucepan of lightly salted water to the boil. Add the pasta, return to the boil and cook for 8–10 minutes, or until tender but still firm to the bite. Drain well and transfer to a warmed serving dish. Add the remaining olive oil and toss. Add the sauce and toss again. Sprinkle with parsley and serve immediately with mixed salad leaves.

SERVES 6

1 potato, diced

400 g/14 oz minced steak

1 onion, finely chopped

1 egg

4 tbsp chopped fresh flat-leaf parsley

plain flour, for dusting

5 tbsp extra virgin olive oil

400 ml/14 fl oz passata

2 tbsp tomato purée

400 g/14 oz dried spaghetti

salt and pepper

6 fresh basil leaves, shredded

freshly grated Parmesan cheese,
    to garnish

Spaghetti with Meatballs

The humble meatball, served American-Italian style over spaghetti or tagliatelle, is elevated here to greater heights by using fresh minced steak. The meatballs are tender and succulent and enjoyed by children and adults alike.

• Place the potato in a small saucepan, add cold water to cover and a pinch of salt and bring to the boil. Cook for 10–15 minutes until tender, then drain. Either mash thoroughly with a potato masher or fork or pass through a potato ricer.

• Combine the potato, steak, onion, egg and parsley in a bowl and season to taste with salt and pepper. Spread out the flour on a plate. With dampened hands, shape the meat mixture into walnut-sized balls and roll in the flour. Shake off any excess.

• Heat the olive oil in a heavy-based frying pan, add the meatballs and cook over a medium heat, stirring and turning frequently, for 8–10 minutes, or until golden all over.

• Add the passata and tomato purée and cook for a further 10 minutes, or until the sauce is reduced and thickened.

• Meanwhile, bring a large saucepan of lightly salted water to the boil. Add the pasta, return to the boil and cook for 8–10 minutes, or until tender but still firm to the bite.

• Drain well and add to the meatball sauce, tossing well to coat. Transfer to a warmed serving dish, garnish with the basil leaves and grated Parmesan cheese and serve immediately.

SERVES 4

40 g/1½ oz dried porcini mushrooms

175 ml/6 fl oz hot water

800 g/1 lb 12 oz canned chopped
   tomatoes

1 fresh red chilli, deseeded and finely
   chopped

3 tbsp olive oil

350 g/12 oz skinless, boneless
   chicken, cut into thin strips

2 garlic cloves, finely chopped

350 g/12 oz dried pappardelle

salt and pepper

2 tbsp chopped fresh flat-leaf parsley,
   to garnish

Pappardelle with Chicken & Porcini

Wild mushrooms are used extensively in Italian dishes and porcini mushrooms are the most popular. When using porcini, always soak them first in hot water for 30 minutes, then drain well before cooking.

• Place the porcini in a small bowl, add the hot water and leave to soak for 30 minutes. Meanwhile, place the tomatoes and their can juices in a heavy-based saucepan and break them up with a wooden spoon, then stir in the chilli. Bring to the boil, reduce the heat and simmer, stirring occasionally, for 30 minutes, or until reduced.

• Remove the mushrooms from their soaking liquid with a slotted spoon, reserving the liquid. Strain the liquid through a coffee filter paper or muslin-lined sieve into the tomatoes and simmer for a further 15 minutes. Meanwhile, heat 2 tablespoons of the olive oil in a heavy-based frying pan. Add the chicken and cook, stirring frequently, until golden brown all over and tender. Stir in the mushrooms and garlic and cook for a further 5 minutes.

• While the chicken is cooking, bring a large, heavy-based saucepan of lightly salted water to the boil. Add the pasta, return to the boil and cook for 8–10 minutes, or until tender but still firm to the bite. Drain well, transfer to a warmed serving dish, drizzle with the remaining olive oil and toss lightly. Stir the chicken mixture into the tomato sauce, season to taste with salt and pepper and spoon on to the pasta. Toss lightly, sprinkle with parsley and serve immediately.

SERVES 4

450 g/1 lb dried spaghetti

1 tbsp olive oil

225 g/8 oz rindless pancetta or
streaky bacon, chopped

4 eggs

5 tbsp single cream

4 tbsp freshly grated Parmesan
cheese

salt and pepper

Spaghetti alla Carbonara

For a more substantial dish, cook 1–2 finely chopped shallots with the pancetta and add 115 g/4 oz sliced mushrooms after 4 minutes, then continue as above.

• Bring a large, heavy-based saucepan of lightly salted water to the boil. Add the pasta, return to the boil and cook for 8–10 minutes, or until tender but still firm to the bite.

• Meanwhile, heat the olive oil in a heavy-based frying pan. Add the chopped pancetta and cook over a medium heat, stirring frequently, for 8–10 minutes.

• Beat the eggs with the cream in a small bowl and season to taste with salt and pepper. Drain the pasta and return it to the saucepan. Tip in the contents of the frying pan, then add the egg mixture and half the Parmesan cheese. Stir well, then transfer to a warmed serving dish. Serve immediately, sprinkled with the remaining cheese.

SERVES 4

1 kg/2 lb 4 oz live clams

175 ml/6 fl oz water

175 ml/6 fl oz dry white wine

350 g/12 oz dried spaghetti

5 tbsp olive oil

2 garlic cloves, finely chopped

4 tbsp chopped fresh flat-leaf parsley

salt and pepper

Spaghetti with Clams

In Italy, this dish would be prepared with small, smooth-shelled clams, known as vongole, but you can use other varieties, such as Venus clams. If fresh clams are not available, substitute with 280 g/10 oz of clams in brine, which are sold in jars.

• Scrub the clams under cold running water and discard any with broken or damaged shells or any that do not shut when sharply tapped. Place the clams in a large, heavy-based saucepan, add the water and wine, cover and cook over a high heat, shaking the saucepan occasionally, for 5 minutes, or until the shells have opened.

• Remove the clams with a slotted spoon and leave to cool slightly. Strain the cooking liquid through a muslin-lined sieve into a small saucepan. Bring to the boil and cook until reduced by about half, then remove from the heat. Meanwhile, discard any clams that have not opened, remove the remainder from their shells and reserve until required.

• Bring a large saucepan of lightly salted water to the boil. Add the pasta, return to the boil and cook for 8–10 minutes, or until tender but still firm to the bite.

• Meanwhile, heat the olive oil in a large, heavy-based frying pan. Add the garlic and cook, stirring frequently, for 2 minutes. Add the parsley and the reduced cooking liquid and simmer gently.

• Drain the pasta and add it to the frying pan with the clams. Season to taste with salt and pepper and cook, stirring constantly, for 4 minutes, or until the pasta is coated and the clams have heated through. Transfer to a warmed serving dish and serve immediately.

SERVES 4

450 g/1 lb dried tagliatelle

fresh basil sprigs, to garnish

PESTO

2 garlic cloves

25 g/1 oz pine kernels

115 g/4 oz fresh basil leaves

55 g/2 oz freshly grated
   Parmesan cheese

125 ml/4 fl oz olive oil

salt

Pasta with Pesto

To store pesto, place it in a screw-top jar, cover the surface with a layer of olive oil and keep in the refrigerator for up to 2 weeks.

• To make the pesto, put the garlic, pine kernels, a large pinch of salt and the basil into a mortar and pound to a paste with a pestle. Transfer to a bowl and gradually work in the Parmesan cheese with a wooden spoon, followed by the olive oil to make a thick, creamy sauce. Taste, and adjust the seasoning if necessary.

• Alternatively, put the garlic, pine kernels and a large pinch of salt into a blender or food processor and process briefly. Add the basil leaves and process to a paste. With the motor still running, gradually add the olive oil. Scrape into a bowl and beat in the cheese. Season to taste with salt.

• Bring a large saucepan of lightly salted water to the boil. Add the pasta, return to the boil and cook for 8–10 minutes, or until tender but still firm to the bite. Drain well, return to the saucepan and toss with half the pesto, then divide between warmed serving plates and top with the remaining pesto. Garnish with basil sprigs and serve.

SERVES 4

150 ml/5 fl oz dry white wine

1 tbsp sun-dried tomato paste

2 fresh red chillies

2 garlic cloves, finely chopped

350 g/12 oz dried tortiglioni

4 tbsp chopped fresh flat-leaf parsley

salt and pepper

pecorino cheese shavings, to garnish

SUGOCASA

5 tbsp extra virgin olive oil

450 g/1 lb plum tomatoes, chopped

salt and pepper

Hot Chilli Pasta

If time is short, use ready-made sugocasa, available from most supermarkets and sometimes labelled crushed tomatoes. Failing that, you could use passata, but the sauce will be thinner.

• First make the sugocasa. Heat the olive oil in a frying pan until it is almost smoking. Add the tomatoes and cook over a high heat for 2–3 minutes. Reduce the heat to low and cook gently for 20 minutes, or until very soft. Season with salt and pepper, then pass through a sieve or process in a blender and put into a clean saucepan.

• Add the wine, sun-dried tomato paste, whole chillies and garlic to the sugocasa and bring to the boil. Reduce the heat and simmer gently.

• Meanwhile, bring a large saucepan of lightly salted water to the boil. Add the pasta, return to the boil and cook for 8–10 minutes, or until tender but still firm to the bite.

• Meanwhile, remove the chillies and taste the sauce. If you prefer a hotter flavour, chop some or all of the chillies and return them to the saucepan. Check the seasoning at the same time, then stir in half the parsley.

• Drain the pasta and tip it into a warmed serving bowl. Add the sauce and toss to coat. Sprinkle with the remaining parsley, garnish with the pecorino shavings and serve immediately.

SERVES 4

55 g/2 oz unsalted butter

115 g/4 oz white onions or shallots,
    very finely chopped

800 g/1 lb 12 oz pumpkin, unprepared
    weight

pinch of freshly grated nutmeg

350 g/12 oz dried radiatori

200 ml/7 fl oz single cream

4 tbsp freshly grated Parmesan
    cheese, plus extra to serve

2 tbsp chopped fresh flat-leaf parsley

salt and pepper

Radiatori with Pumpkin Sauce

Although traditionally made with pumpkin, you could also use butternut or acorn squash for this dish.

• Melt the butter in a heavy-based saucepan over a low heat. Add the onions, sprinkle with a little salt, cover and cook, stirring frequently, for 25–30 minutes.

• Scoop out and discard the seeds from the pumpkin. Peel and finely chop the flesh. Tip the pumpkin into the saucepan and season to taste with nutmeg. Cover and cook over a low heat, stirring occasionally, for 45 minutes.

• Meanwhile, bring a large saucepan of lightly salted water to the boil. Add the pasta, return to the boil and cook for 8–10 minutes, or until tender but still firm to the bite. Drain thoroughly, reserving about 150 ml/5 fl oz of the cooking liquid.

• Stir the cream, grated Parmesan cheese and parsley into the pumpkin sauce and season to taste with salt and pepper. If the mixture seems a little too thick, add some or all of the reserved cooking liquid and stir. Tip in the pasta and toss for 1 minute. Serve immediately, with extra Parmesan cheese for sprinkling.

SERVES 6

350 g/12 oz dried fusilli

3 tbsp olive oil

350 g/12 oz wild mushrooms or
    button mushrooms, sliced

1 garlic clove, finely chopped

400 ml/14 fl oz double cream

250 g/9 oz Gorgonzola cheese,
    crumbled

salt and pepper

2 tbsp chopped fresh flat-leaf parsley,
    to garnish

Fusilli with Gorgonzola & Mushroom Sauce

Wild mushrooms have a much earthier flavour than cultivated ones, so they complement the strong taste of the cheese. If you can find them, Porcini are especially delicious, but rather expensive. Field or Caesar's mushrooms would also be a good choice. Otherwise, use cultivated mushrooms, but add 25 g/1 oz dried porcini, soaked for 30 minutes in 225 ml/8 fl oz hot water.

• Bring a large saucepan of lightly salted water to the boil. Add the pasta, return to the boil and cook for 8–10 minutes, or until tender but still firm to the bite.

• Meanwhile, heat the olive oil in a heavy-based saucepan. Add the mushrooms and cook over a low heat, stirring frequently, for 5 minutes. Add the garlic and cook for a further 2 minutes.

• Add the cream, bring to the boil and cook for 1 minute until slightly thickened. Stir in the cheese and cook over a low heat until it has melted. Do not allow the sauce to boil once the cheese has been added. Season to taste with salt and pepper and remove the saucepan from the heat.

• Drain the pasta and tip it into the sauce. Toss well to coat, then serve immediately, garnished with the parsley.

The majority of baked pasta dishes, including well known favourites such as lasagne and macaroni cheese, are made in a similar way: the ingredients are prepared or cooked separately and then assembled in the dish just before baking in the oven. Pasta, accompanied by other ingredients such as meat, cheese or vegetables typically make up a baked pasta dish, and the dish is usually prepared with a sauce. One element of these dishes that you will need to prepare time and time again is Béchamel Sauce. For this reason it has been included on page 9 for easy reference.

The Italians have a name for these baked dishes – they call it pasticci. Many baked pasta dishes were traditionally served at banquets as far back as the eighteenth century. In the past, they were known as 'timballi', but today the word 'timballo' is used to

BAKED TO PERFECTION

describe a baked dish that is served turned out of its dish.

The baked pasta dishes included in this section are substantial and are therefore suitable for serving as a main meal. They are also ideal for buffet parties when catering for a large number of people, as they are easy to serve and can be eaten with just a fork. An additional advantage is that they can be prepared in advance. All that is needed to accompany them is a fresh green salad, and some crusty or garlic bread.

SERVES 4

3 tbsp olive oil

1 onion, finely chopped

1 celery stick, finely chopped

1 carrot, finely chopped

100 g/3½ oz pancetta or rindless
   streaky bacon, finely chopped

175 g/6 oz fresh beef mince

175 g/6 oz fresh pork mince

100 ml/3½ fl oz dry red wine

150 ml/5 fl oz beef stock

1 tbsp tomato purée

1 clove

1 bay leaf

150 ml/5 fl oz boiling milk

400 g/14 oz dried lasagne

55 g/2 oz unsalted butter, diced,
   plus extra for greasing

300 ml/10 fl oz Béchamel Sauce

140 g/5 oz mozzarella cheese, diced

140 g/5 oz freshly grated Parmesan
   cheese

salt and pepper

Baked Lasagne

This classic Italian dish is a speciality of the Emilia-Romagna region, the gastronomic centre of Italy. It can be made with dried or fresh lasagne and either verdi (spinach) or egg lasagne. You could also use all minced beef or all minced pork if wished.

• Heat the olive oil in a large, heavy-based saucepan. Add the onion, celery, carrot, pancetta, beef and pork and cook over a medium heat, stirring frequently and breaking up the meat with a wooden spoon, for 10 minutes, or until lightly browned.

• Add the wine, bring to the boil and cook until reduced. Add about two thirds of the stock, bring to the boil and cook until reduced. Combine the remaining stock and tomato purée and add to the saucepan. Season to taste with salt and pepper, add the clove and bay leaf and pour in the milk. Cover and leave to simmer over a low heat for 1½ hours.

• Preheat the oven to 200°C/400°F/Gas Mark 6. Unless you are using lasagne that needs no precooking, bring a large, heavy-based saucepan of lightly salted water to the boil. Add the lasagne sheets, in batches, return to the boil and cook for about 10 minutes, or until tender but still firm to the bite. Remove with tongs and spread out on a clean tea towel. Remove the meat sauce from the heat and discard the clove and bay leaf.

• Lightly grease a large, ovenproof dish with butter. Place a layer of lasagne in the base and cover it with a layer of meat sauce. Spoon a layer of Béchamel Sauce on top and sprinkle with one third of the mozzarella and Parmesan cheeses. Continue making layers until all the ingredients are used, ending with a topping of Béchamel Sauce and sprinkled cheese.

• Dot the top of the lasagne with the diced butter and bake in the preheated oven for 30 minutes, or until golden and bubbling.

SERVES 4

2 tbsp olive oil

1 onion, chopped

1 garlic clove, finely chopped

2 carrots, diced

55 g/2 oz pancetta or rindless streaky
    bacon, chopped

115 g/4 oz mushrooms, chopped

450 g/1 lb fresh pork mince

125 ml/4 fl oz dry white wine

4 tbsp passata

200 g/7 oz canned chopped tomatoes

2 tsp chopped fresh sage or
    ½ tsp dried sage

225 g/8 oz dried elicoidali

140 g/5 oz mozzarella cheese, diced

4 tbsp freshly grated Parmesan
    cheese

300 ml/10 fl oz hot Béchamel Sauce

salt and pepper

Pork & Pasta Bake

When cooking with olive oil, there is no need to use extra virgin olive oil as the flavour will be lost during cooking. Olive oil is best stored in a cool place, out of direct sunlight. Do not store in the refrigerator.

• Preheat the oven to 200°C/400°F/Gas Mark 6. Heat the olive oil in a large, heavy-based frying pan. Add the onion, garlic and carrots and cook over a low heat, stirring occasionally, for 5 minutes, or until the onion has softened. Add the pancetta and cook for 5 minutes. Add the chopped mushrooms and cook, stirring occasionally, for a further 2 minutes. Add the pork and cook, breaking it up with a wooden spoon, until the meat is browned all over. Stir in the wine, passata, chopped tomatoes and their can juices and the sage. Season to taste with salt and pepper, bring to the boil, then cover and simmer over a low heat for 25–30 minutes.

• Meanwhile, bring a large, heavy-based saucepan of lightly salted water to the boil. Add the pasta, return to the boil and cook for 8–10 minutes, or until tender but still firm to the bite.

• Spoon the pork mixture into a large ovenproof dish. Stir the mozzarella and half the Parmesan cheese into the Béchamel Sauce. Drain the pasta and stir the sauce into it, then spoon it over the pork mixture. Sprinkle with the remaining Parmesan cheese and bake in the oven for 25–30 minutes, or until golden brown. Serve immediately.

SERVES 6

70 g/2½ oz butter, plus extra
    for greasing

350 g/12 oz dried spaghetti

200 g/7 oz smoked salmon, cut into
    strips

280 g/10 oz large Mediterranean
    prawns or tiger prawns, cooked,
    peeled and deveined

300 ml/10 fl oz Béchamel Sauce

115 g/4 oz freshly grated Parmesan
    cheese

salt

Layered Spaghetti with Smoked Salmon & Prawns

This dish would also
be delicious made with
smoked halibut instead of
the salmon and smoked
mussels instead of
the prawns.

• Preheat the oven to 180°C/350°F/Gas Mark 4. Grease a large, ovenproof dish and reserve.
• Bring a large saucepan of lightly salted water to the boil. Add the pasta, return to the boil and cook for 8–10 minutes, or until tender but still firm to the bite. Drain well, return to the saucepan, add 55 g/2 oz of the butter and toss well.
• Spoon half the spaghetti into the prepared dish, cover with the strips of smoked salmon, then top with the prawns. Pour over half the Béchamel Sauce and sprinkle with half the Parmesan. Add the remaining spaghetti, cover with the remaining sauce and sprinkle with the remaining Parmesan. Dice the remaining butter and dot it over the surface.
• Bake in the preheated oven for 15 minutes, or until the top is golden. Serve immediately.

SERVES 4

350 g/12 oz dried short-cut macaroni

85 g/3 oz butter, plus extra
    for greasing

2 small fennel bulbs, thinly sliced

175 g/6 oz mushrooms, thinly sliced

175 g/6 oz cooked peeled prawns

pinch of cayenne pepper

300 ml/10 fl oz Béchamel Sauce

55 g/2 oz freshly grated Parmesan
    cheese

2 large tomatoes, sliced

olive oil, for brushing

1 tsp dried oregano

salt and pepper

Macaroni & Seafood Bake

Fennel imparts a delicate aniseed flavour to dishes and goes very well with fish. To prepare the fennel bulbs, cut off the stalk and root end, then slice the bulbs lengthways.

• Preheat the oven to 180°C/350°F/Gas Mark 4. Bring a large saucepan of lightly salted water to the boil. Add the pasta, return to the boil and cook for 8–10 minutes, or until tender but still firm to the bite. Drain and return to the saucepan. Add 25 g/1 oz of the butter to the pasta, cover, shake the saucepan and keep warm.

• Melt the remaining butter in a separate saucepan. Add the fennel and fry for 3–4 minutes. Stir in the mushrooms and fry for a further 2 minutes. Stir in the prawns, then remove the saucepan from the heat. Stir the cayenne pepper into the Béchamel Sauce and add the prawn mixture and pasta.

• Grease a large ovenproof dish with butter, then pour the mixture into the dish and spread evenly. Sprinkle over the Parmesan cheese and arrange the tomato slices in a ring around the edge. Brush the tomatoes with olive oil, then sprinkle over the oregano. Bake in the preheated oven for 25 minutes, or until golden brown. Serve immediately.

SERVES 6

350 g/12 oz dried conchiglie

85 g/3 oz butter, plus extra for
    greasing

2 fennel bulbs, thinly sliced

175 g/6 oz mushrooms, thinly sliced

175 g/6 oz cooked peeled prawns

175 g/6 oz cooked crabmeat

pinch of cayenne pepper

300 ml/10 fl oz Béchamel Sauce

55 g/2 oz freshly grated Parmesan
    cheese

2 beef tomatoes, sliced

olive oil, for brushing

salt

green salad and crusty bread, to serve

Shellfish Bake

You can use either cooked fresh crabmeat or canned. If you wish to use fresh crab and time is limited, buy a ready-dressed crab from your fishmonger.

• Preheat the oven to 180°C/350°F/Gas Mark 4. Bring a large, heavy-based saucepan of lightly salted water to the boil. Add the pasta, return to the boil and cook for 8–10 minutes, or until tender but still firm to the bite. Drain well, return to the saucepan and stir in 25 g/1 oz of the butter. Cover the pan and keep warm.

• Meanwhile, melt the remaining butter in a large, heavy-based frying pan. Add the fennel and cook over a medium heat for 5 minutes, or until softened. Stir in the mushrooms and cook for a further 2 minutes. Stir in the prawns and crabmeat, cook for a further 1 minute, then remove the frying pan from the heat.

• Grease 6 small ovenproof dishes with butter. Stir the cayenne pepper into the Béchamel Sauce, add the shellfish mixture and pasta, then spoon into the prepared dishes. Sprinkle with the Parmesan cheese and arrange the tomato slices on top, then brush the tomatoes with a little olive oil.

• Bake in the preheated oven for 25 minutes, or until golden brown. Serve hot with a green salad and crusty bread.

SERVES 4

1 crab, about 1.5 kg/ 3 lb 5 oz,
     freshly cooked
2 tbsp extra virgin olive oil
2 fresh red chillies, deseeded and
     finely chopped
4 garlic cloves, finely chopped

800 g/1 lb 12 oz canned tomatoes
225 ml/8 fl oz dry white wine
350 g/12 oz dried spaghetti
450 g/1 lb live mussels
2 tbsp butter
115 g/4 oz prepared squid, sliced

175 g/6 oz raw Mediterranean prawns
3 tbsp roughly chopped fresh flat-leaf
     parsley
1 tbsp shredded fresh basil leaves
salt and pepper

Seafood Pasta Parcels

Although not a long-standing tradition, baking parcels of mixed ingredients in the oven has now become a favourite Italian cooking technique. It is especially well suited to seafood, as it seals in the moisture and keeps it tender.

• Holding the crab upright with one hand, bang firmly on the underside of the shell with your clenched fist to loosen the body. Then, with the shell towards you and still holding it upright, force the body away from the shell by pushing with your thumbs. Twist off and discard the tail. Twist off the legs and claws. Crack them open and remove all the meat.

• Pull off and discard the gills – dead man's fingers – then split open the body down the centre using a sharp knife. Remove all the meat, discarding any pieces of shell. Reserve all the shell and set aside the crabmeat. Carefully break up the larger pieces of shell with a meat mallet or the end of a rolling pin.

• Heat 1 tablespoon of the olive oil in a large saucepan. Add half the chillies and half the garlic, then add the pieces of crab shell. Cook over a medium heat, stirring occasionally, for 2–3 minutes. Add the tomatoes with their can juices and the wine. Reduce the heat and simmer for about 1 hour. Pass the sauce through a sieve, pressing down with a wooden spoon. Season to taste with salt and pepper and reserve.

• Preheat the oven to 180°C/350°F/Gas Mark 4. Bring a large saucepan of lightly salted water to the boil. Add the pasta, return to the boil and cook for 8–10 minutes, until tender but still firm to the bite.

• Scrub and debeard the mussels under cold running water. Discard any damaged or broken ones and any that do not shut immediately when sharply tapped. Heat the remaining olive oil with the butter in a large, heavy-based saucepan. Add the remaining chilli and garlic and cook over a low heat, stirring occasionally, for 5 minutes, or until softened. Add the squid, prawns and mussels, cover and cook over a high heat for 4–5 minutes, or until the mussels have opened. Remove the saucepan from the heat and discard any mussels that remain closed.

• Drain the pasta and add it to the seafood with the chilli and tomato sauce, parsley and basil, tossing well to coat. Cut out 4 large squares of baking paper or greaseproof paper. Divide the pasta and seafood between them, placing it on one half of each sheet. Fold over the other half and turn in the edges securely to seal. Transfer to a large baking sheet and bake in the preheated oven for 10 minutes, or until the parcels have puffed up. Serve immediately.

SERVES 4

olive oil, for brushing

2 aubergines, sliced

25 g/1 oz butter

1 garlic clove, finely chopped

4 courgettes, sliced

1 tbsp finely chopped fresh flat-leaf
    parsley

1 tbsp finely chopped fresh marjoram

225 g/8 oz mozzarella cheese, grated

600 ml/1 pint passata

175 g/6 oz dried no-pre-cook lasagne

salt and pepper

600 ml/1 pint Béchamel Sauce

55 g/2 oz freshly grated Parmesan
    cheese

Vegetarian Lasagne

Make sure that the oiled griddle pan is very hot before adding the aubergine slices. Add extra oil if the aubergines are sticking to the pan.

• Preheat the oven to 200°C/400°F/Gas Mark 6. Brush a large ovenproof dish with olive oil. Brush a large griddle pan with olive oil and heat until smoking. Add half the aubergines and cook over a medium heat for 8 minutes, or until golden brown all over. Remove the aubergines from the griddle pan and drain on kitchen paper. Add the remaining slices and extra oil, if necessary, and cook for 8 minutes, or until golden brown all over.

• Melt the butter in a frying pan and add the garlic, courgettes, parsley and marjoram. Cook over a medium heat, stirring frequently, for 5 minutes, or until the courgettes are golden brown all over. Remove from the frying pan and leave to drain on kitchen paper.

• Layer the aubergines, courgettes, mozzarella, passata and lasagne in the dish, seasoning with salt and pepper as you go and finishing with a layer of lasagne. Pour over the Béchamel Sauce, making sure that all the pasta is covered. Sprinkle with the grated Parmesan cheese and bake in the preheated oven for 30–40 minutes, or until golden brown. Serve immediately.

SERVES 4

140 g/5 oz fontina cheese, thinly
    sliced
300 ml/10 fl oz hot Béchamel Sauce
85 g/3 oz butter, plus extra for
    greasing
350 g/12 oz mixed wild mushrooms,
    sliced

350 g/12 oz dried tagliatelle
2 egg yolks
4 tbsp freshly grated pecorino cheese
salt and pepper
mixed salad leaves, to serve

Baked Pasta with Mushrooms

A bake of pasta, béchamel sauce and a tasty filling is sometimes called a crostada.

- Preheat the oven to 200°C/400°F/Gas Mark 6. Stir the fontina cheese into the Béchamel Sauce and reserve.
- Melt 25 g/1 oz of the butter in a large saucepan. Add the mushrooms and cook over a low heat, stirring occasionally, for 10 minutes.
- Meanwhile, bring a large saucepan of lightly salted water to the boil. Add the pasta, return to the boil and cook for 8–10 minutes, or until tender but still firm to the bite. Drain, return to the saucepan and add the remaining butter, the egg yolks and about one third of the sauce, then season to taste with salt and pepper. Toss well to mix, then gently stir in the mushrooms.
- Lightly grease a large, ovenproof dish with butter and spoon in the pasta mixture. Evenly pour over the remaining sauce and sprinkle with the grated pecorino cheese. Bake in the preheated oven for 15–20 minutes, or until golden brown. Serve immediately with mixed salad leaves.

Little filled parcels of pasta, such as small or large squares or rounds of ravioli, large squares of tortelloni, rings of tortellini and crescents of agnolotti, along with stuffed tubes of cannelloni and rigatoni, are all types of filled pasta. These pastas are filled with a variety of ingredients, such as meat, fish, vegetables or cheese. Filled pastas all originate in specific areas of northern and central Italy where a good supply of eggs was available to make a moist dough, suitable for stuffing. This tradition was not common in southern Italy, which is better known for originating dried pasta.

You will need to make the Basic Pasta Dough recipe (see page 9) for many of the dishes in this chapter. The secret of success for making filled pasta is not to let the dough dry out too much once it has been made but to proceed with the recipe. Also, roll out the

FLAVOUR-FILLED

dough thinly, so that the shapes are not too heavy, but not so thinly that the shapes will split. Do not overfill them or they will burst when they are cooked. After making the parcels, they can be left on a clean, floured tea towel for about an hour, turning them once, so that they become less sticky on both sides. When it comes to cooking filled pasta, try to avoid overcooking as they may split open, which would be a pity after all your creativity!

SERVES 4

butter, for greasing

2 tbsp olive oil

2 garlic cloves, crushed

1 large onion, finely chopped

225 g/8 oz wild mushrooms, sliced

350 g/12 oz fresh chicken mince

115 g/4 oz prosciutto, diced

150 ml/5 fl oz Marsala wine

200 g/7 oz canned chopped tomatoes

1 tbsp shredded fresh basil leaves

2 tbsp tomato purée

10–12 dried cannelloni tubes

600 ml/1 pint Béchamel sauce

85 g/3 oz freshly grated Parmesan
cheese

salt and pepper

Chicken & Wild Mushroom Cannelloni

You can use any combination of wild mushrooms. For extra flavour, add 25 g/1 oz dried porcini, soaked in hot water for 30 minutes.

• Preheat the oven to 190°C/375°F/Gas Mark 5. Lightly grease a large ovenproof dish. Heat the olive oil in a heavy-based frying pan. Add the garlic, onion and mushrooms and cook over a low heat, stirring frequently, for 8–10 minutes. Add the chicken mince and prosciutto and cook, stirring frequently, for 12 minutes, or until browned all over. Stir in the Marsala, tomatoes and their can juices, basil and tomato purée and cook for 4 minutes. Season to taste with salt and pepper, then cover and simmer for 30 minutes. Uncover, stir and simmer for 15 minutes.

• Meanwhile, bring a large, heavy-based saucepan of lightly salted water to the boil. Add the pasta, return to the boil and cook for 8–10 minutes, or until tender but still firm to the bite. Using a slotted spoon, transfer the cannelloni tubes to a plate and pat dry with kitchen paper.

• Using a teaspoon, fill the cannelloni tubes with the chicken, prosciutto and mushroom mixture. Transfer them to the ovenproof dish. Pour over the Béchamel Sauce to cover them completely and sprinkle with the grated Parmesan cheese.

• Bake the cannelloni in the preheated oven for 30 minutes, or until golden brown and bubbling. Serve immediately.

SERVES 4

115 g/4 oz boned chicken breast, skinned

55 g/2 oz Parma ham

40 g/1½ oz cooked spinach, well drained

1 tbsp finely chopped onion

2 tbsp freshly grated Parmesan cheese

pinch of ground allspice

1 egg, beaten

450 g/1 lb Basic Pasta Dough

salt and pepper

2 tbsp chopped fresh flat-leaf parsley, to garnish

SAUCE

300 ml/10 fl oz single cream

2 garlic cloves, crushed

115 g/4 oz button mushrooms, thinly sliced

4 tbsp freshly grated Parmesan cheese

salt and pepper

Chicken Tortellini

Think ahead by making double the quantity of filled tortellini. What you don't use will keep in the refrigerator for up to three days and can be used for a quick mid-week supper or snack.

• Bring a saucepan of lightly salted water to the boil. Add the chicken and poach for 10 minutes. Leave to cool slightly, then put in a food processor with the Parma ham, spinach and onion and process until finely chopped. Stir in the Parmesan cheese, allspice and egg and season to taste with salt and pepper.

• Thinly roll out the Pasta Dough and cut into 4–5-cm/1½–2-inch rounds. Place ½ teaspoon of the chicken and ham filling in the centre of each round. Fold the pieces in half and press the edges to seal, then wrap each piece around your index finger, cross over the ends and curl the rest of the dough backwards to make a navel shape. Re-roll the trimmings and repeat until all of the dough is used up.

• Bring a saucepan of salted water to the boil. Add the tortellini, in batches, return to the boil and cook for 5 minutes. Drain the tortellini well and transfer to a serving dish.

• To make the sauce, bring the cream and garlic to a boil in a small saucepan, then simmer for 3 minutes. Add the mushrooms and half the cheese, season to taste with salt and pepper and simmer for 2–3 minutes. Pour the sauce over the tortellini. Sprinkle over the remaining Parmesan cheese, garnish with the parsley and serve.

SERVES 4

2 tbsp olive oil

2 onions, chopped

2 garlic cloves, finely chopped

1 tbsp shredded fresh basil

800 g/1 lb 12 oz canned chopped
    tomatoes

1 tbsp tomato purée

350 g/12 oz dried cannelloni tubes

butter, for greasing

225 g/8 oz ricotta cheese

115 g/4 oz cooked ham, diced

1 egg

55 g/2 oz freshly grated pecorino
    cheese

salt and pepper

Cannelloni with Ham & Ricotta

Make sure that the cooked cannelloni tubes are dry before filling, as they may go soggy during cooking. Pat dry thoroughly with kitchen paper before filling with the ham and ricotta mixture.

• Preheat the oven to 180°C/350°F/Gas Mark 4. Heat the olive oil in a large, heavy-based frying pan. Add the onions and garlic and cook over a low heat, stirring occasionally, for 5 minutes, or until the onion is softened.

• Add the basil, chopped tomatoes and their can juices and the tomato purée and season to taste with salt and pepper. Reduce the heat and leave to simmer for 30 minutes, or until thickened.

• Meanwhile, bring a large, heavy-based saucepan of lightly salted water to the boil. Add the cannelloni tubes, return to the boil and cook for 8–10 minutes, or until tender but still firm to the bite. Using a slotted spoon, transfer the cannelloni tubes to a large plate and pat dry with kitchen paper.

• Grease a large, shallow ovenproof dish with butter. Mix the ricotta, ham and egg together in a bowl and season to taste with salt and pepper. Using a teaspoon, fill the cannelloni tubes with the ricotta, ham and egg mixture and place in a single layer in the dish. Pour the tomato sauce over the cannelloni and sprinkle with the grated pecorino cheese. Bake in the preheated oven for 30 minutes, or until golden brown. Serve immediately.

SERVES 4

115 g/4 oz cooked skinless, boneless
    chicken breast, roughly chopped
55 g/2 oz cooked spinach
55 g/2 oz prosciutto, roughly chopped
1 shallot, roughly chopped
6 tbsp freshly grated pecorino cheese

pinch of freshly grated nutmeg
2 eggs, lightly beaten
1 quantity Basic Pasta Dough
plain white flour, for dusting
300 ml/10 fl oz double cream or panna
    da cucina
2 garlic cloves, finely chopped

115 g/4 oz chestnut mushrooms,
    thinly sliced
2 tbsp shredded fresh basil
salt and pepper
fresh basil sprigs, to garnish

Creamy Chicken Ravioli

To cook the chicken breast, place it in a saucepan with 1 tablespoon lemon juice and just enough water to cover. Season to taste with salt and pepper and poach gently for 10 minutes, or until cooked.

• Place the chicken, spinach, prosciutto and shallot in a food processor and process until chopped and blended. Transfer to a bowl, stir in 2 tablespoons of the cheese, the nutmeg and half the egg. Season with salt and pepper.

• Halve the Pasta Dough. Wrap one piece in clingfilm and thinly roll out the other on a lightly floured work surface. Cover with a tea towel and roll out the second piece of dough. Place small mounds of the filling in rows 4 cm/1½ inches apart on one sheet of dough and brush the spaces in between with beaten egg. Lift the second piece of dough to fit on top. Press down firmly between the mounds of filling, pushing out any air. Cut into squares and place on a floured tea towel. Leave the ravioli to rest for 1 hour.

• Bring a large saucepan of lightly salted water to the boil. Add the ravioli, in batches, return to the boil and cook for 5 minutes. Remove with a slotted spoon and drain on kitchen paper, then transfer to a warmed dish.

• Meanwhile, to make the sauce pour the cream into a frying pan, add the garlic and bring to the boil. Simmer for 1 minute, then add the mushrooms and 2 tablespoons of the remaining cheese. Season to taste and simmer for 3 minutes. Stir in the basil, then pour the sauce over the ravioli. Sprinkle with the remaining cheese, garnish with basil sprigs and serve.

SERVES 4

butter, for greasing

450 g/1 lb dried rigatoni

115 g/4 oz sun-dried tomatoes,
    drained and sliced

FILLING

200 g/7 oz canned flaked tuna, drained

225 g/8 oz ricotta cheese

SAUCE

125 ml/4 fl oz double cream

225 g/8 oz freshly grated Parmesan
    cheese

salt and pepper

Baked Tuna & Ricotta Rigatoni

For a vegetarian alternative to this recipe, simply substitute a mixture of stoned and chopped black olives and chopped walnuts for the tuna. Follow exactly the same cooking method.

• Preheat the oven to 200°C/400°F/Gas Mark 6. Lightly grease a large ovenproof dish with butter. Bring a large, heavy-based saucepan of lightly salted water to the boil. Add the rigatoni, return to the boil and cook for 8–10 minutes, or until just tender but still firm to the bite. Drain the pasta and leave until cool enough to handle.

• Meanwhile, mix the tuna and ricotta cheese together in a bowl to form a soft paste. Spoon the mixture into a piping bag and use to fill the rigatoni. Arrange the filled pasta tubes side by side in the prepared dish.

• To make the sauce, mix the cream and Parmesan cheese together in a bowl and season to taste with salt and pepper. Spoon the sauce over the rigatoni and top with the sun-dried tomatoes, arranged in a criss-cross pattern. Bake in the preheated oven for 20 minutes. Serve hot straight from the dish.

SERVES 4

6 spring onions

350 g/12 oz cooked crabmeat

2 tsp finely chopped fresh root ginger

⅛–¼ tsp chilli or Tabasco sauce

700 g/1 lb 9 oz tomatoes, peeled,
   deseeded and roughly chopped

1 garlic clove, finely chopped

1 tbsp white wine vinegar

1 quantity Basic Pasta Dough

plain flour, for dusting

1 egg, lightly beaten

2 tbsp double cream or panna
   da cucina

salt

shredded spring onion, to garnish

Crab Ravioli

For a change, use tomato-, beetroot- or spinach-flavoured pasta instead of the plain variety.

• Thinly slice the spring onions, keeping the white and green parts separate. Mix the green spring onions, crabmeat, ginger and chilli sauce to taste together in a bowl. Cover with clingfilm and chill.

• Place the tomatoes in a food processor and process to a purée. Place the garlic, white spring onions and vinegar in a saucepan and add the puréed tomatoes. Bring to the boil, stirring frequently, then reduce the heat and simmer gently for 10 minutes. Remove from the heat.

• Halve the Pasta Dough. Wrap one piece in clingfilm and thinly roll out the other on a lightly floured work surface. Cover with a tea towel and roll out the second piece of dough. Place small mounds of the crabmeat mixture in rows 4 cm/1½ inches apart on one sheet of dough and brush the spaces in between with beaten egg. Lift the second piece of dough to fit on top. Press down firmly between the mounds of filling, pushing out any air. Cut into squares, place on a tea towel and leave to rest for 1 hour.

• Bring a large, heavy-based saucepan of lightly salted water to the boil. Add the ravioli, in batches, return to the boil and cook for 5 minutes. Remove with a slotted spoon and drain on kitchen paper. Meanwhile, gently heat the tomato sauce and whisk in the cream. Place the ravioli in serving dishes, pour over the sauce, garnish with shredded spring onion and serve.

SERVES 4

butter, for greasing

1 quantity Basic Pasta Dough

plain flour, for dusting

85 g/3 oz freshly grated Parmesan
cheese

mixed salad leaves,
to serve

FILLING

125 ml/4 fl oz olive oil

1 red onion, chopped

3 garlic cloves, chopped

2 large aubergines, cut into chunks

3 large courgettes, cut into chunks

6 beef tomatoes, peeled, deseeded
and roughly chopped

1 large green pepper, deseeded and
diced

1 large red pepper, deseeded and
diced

1 tbsp sun-dried tomato paste

1 tbsp shredded fresh basil

salt and pepper

Mixed Vegetable Agnolotti

If the filling seems too
sloppy after cooking, boil
uncovered for 1–2 minutes
to reduce slightly. Make
sure that any unused dough
is covered with a tea towel
to prevent it drying out.

• Preheat the oven to 200°C/400°F/Gas Mark 6. To make the filling, heat the olive oil in a large, heavy-based saucepan. Add the onion and garlic and cook over a low heat, stirring occasionally, for 5 minutes, or until softened. Add the aubergines, courgettes, tomatoes, green and red peppers, sun-dried tomato paste and basil. Season to taste with salt and pepper, cover and leave to simmer gently, stirring occasionally, for 20 minutes.

• Lightly grease an ovenproof dish with butter. Roll out the Pasta Dough on a lightly floured work surface and stamp out 7.5-cm/3-inch rounds with a plain pastry cutter. Place a spoonful of the vegetable filling on one side of each round. Dampen the edges slightly and fold the pasta rounds over, pressing together to seal.

• Bring a large saucepan of lightly salted water to the boil. Add the agnolotti, in batches if necessary, return to the boil and cook for 3–4 minutes. Remove with a slotted spoon, drain and transfer to the dish. Sprinkle with the Parmesan cheese and bake in the preheated oven for 20 minutes. Serve with salad leaves.

SERVES 4

350 g/12 oz spinach leaves, coarse
    stalks removed

225 g/8 oz ricotta cheese

55 g/2 oz freshly grated
    Parmesan cheese

2 eggs, lightly beaten

pinch of freshly grated nutmeg

1 quantity Spinach Pasta Dough

plain flour, for dusting

pepper

TO SERVE

freshly grated Parmesan cheese
    (optional)

cheese sauce or tomato sauce
    (optional)

Spinach & Ricotta Ravioli

When cutting the ravioli into squares, use a special pasta cutter available from speciality kitchenware shops. Alternatively, you can use a sharp knife.

• Cook the spinach, with just the water clinging to the leaves after washing, over a low heat for 5 minutes until wilted. Drain and squeeze out as much moisture as possible. Cool, then finely chop. Beat the ricotta cheese until smooth, then stir in the spinach, Parmesan and half the egg and season to taste with nutmeg and pepper.

• Halve the Pasta Dough. Cover one piece and thinly roll out the other on a floured surface. Cover and roll out the second piece. Put small mounds of filling in rows 4 cm/1½ inches apart on one sheet of dough and brush the spaces in between with the remaining beaten egg. Lift the second piece of dough to fit on top. Press down between the mounds, pushing out any air. Cut into squares and rest on a tea towel for 1 hour.

• Bring a large saucepan of salted water to the boil, add the ravioli, in batches, return to the boil and cook for 5 minutes. Remove with a slotted spoon and drain on kitchen paper. Serve with grated Parmesan cheese and/or a sauce, if liked.

Stews and casseroles are the perfect food for when the temperature has dipped outside and it is cold, wet and blustery, or if you simply want a little wholesome comfort food and nothing else will do. This is what this chapter is all about – hearty, filling, satisfying and warming meals for all tastes and appetites.

Stewing is ideal for long, slow cooking. Stews are cooked on the hob, and the heat needs to be gentle so that the liquid is allowed to simmer rather than boil; this can take some fine-tuning. This chapter also includes some classic casseroles. They are very similar to stews, but they are cooked in the oven, not on the hob, and normally have slightly less liquid.

For cooking stews, choose a large, heavy-based saucepan – one that will withstand long, steady

too much meat to seal in one go, then work in two or three batches.

Many of these recipes require a bouquet garni. To make one, take 2 pieces of celery stick, each about 7.5 cm/3 inches long. Lay a good selection of herbs on the inside of one of the celery pieces and place the other on top. Secure firmly with fine kitchen string. Choose from fresh or dried bay leaves and fresh thyme, oregano, parsley, tarragon, mint and chervil sprigs.

Whichever recipe you choose to make from this heart-warming collection, you can rest assured that you will be delighted with the result and will want to cook it again and again, as well as all the other great dishes on offer.

INTRODUCTION TO STEWS & CASSEROLES

cooking without the base burning or buckling, or the food sticking to the base. It should have a tight-fitting lid so that the liquid does not evaporate during cooking. Casseroles require a casserole dish that is both flameproof and ovenproof and has a tight-fitting lid.

When preparing your stew, it is important that any meat is browned and sealed before slow cooking commences. This ensures that the colour, and most importantly the flavour, is preserved rather than leeching out into the liquid. There should be just enough meat to cover the base of the saucepan or frying pan – more could mean uneven sealing and both the flavour and appearance of the dish will be spoilt. If there is

For a dish to be successful, you need to start with the right ingredients. In the case of meat, it is particularly important that the appropriate cut of meat is used for the cooking method involved. Very lean, fine-grain meat is best cooked quickly by being grilled, griddled or fried, whereas coarser cuts, or those with in-built reserves of fat, are ideal for being cooked gently over time in a stew or casserole, resulting in a meltingly tender, fully-flavoured result. Slow cooking also enables the meat flavours to meld with those of the accompanying vegetables, fruit, herbs and spices in the pot.

The recipes in this chapter offer you the opportunity to sample all kinds of delicious combinations, from the simple and hearty to the fruity and fiery. For instance, in Pork Oriental, chunks of pork are teamed with tangy pineapple for a sweet-and-sour taste

MEAT PERFECTION

experience, while Mediterranean Lamb with Apricots & Pistachio Nuts features the warmly spiced mellow fruitiness of North African cuisine. Or choose from Thick Beef & Button Onion Casserole, laced with full-bodied red wine with a touch of zesty orange, or Pork and Vegetable Ragout, a colourful mix of carrots, squash, leeks and okra served with couscous for an exotic twist.

Such variety means that you'll be sure to find a stew or casserole to match your mood, or the season or occasion.

SERVES 6

2 tbsp olive oil

450 g/1 lb button onions, peeled but
    kept whole

2 garlic cloves, halved

900 g/2 lb stewing beef, cubed

½ tsp ground cinnamon

1 tsp ground cloves

1 tsp ground cumin

2 tbsp tomato purée

750 ml full-bodied red wine

grated rind and juice of 1 orange

1 bay leaf

salt and pepper

1 tbsp chopped fresh
flat-leaf parsley, to garnish

boiled or mashed potatoes, to serve

Thick Beef & Button Onion Casserole

If you find it difficult to peel the button onions, bring a large saucepan of water to the boil, then remove from the heat and plunge the onions quickly into the hot water. Remove and plunge into cold water before peeling.

• Preheat the oven to 150°C/300°F/Gas Mark 2. Heat the oil in a large, flameproof casserole and cook the whole onions and garlic, stirring frequently, for 5 minutes, or until softened and beginning to brown. Add the beef and cook over a high heat, stirring frequently, for 5 minutes, or until browned on all sides and sealed.

• Stir the spices and tomato purée into the casserole and add salt and pepper to taste. Pour in the wine, scraping any sediment from the base of the casserole, then add the orange rind and juice and the bay leaf. Bring to the boil and cover.

• Cook in the preheated oven for about 1¼ hours. Remove the lid and cook the casserole for a further hour, stirring once or twice, until the meat is tender. Remove from the oven, garnish with the parsley and serve hot, accompanied by boiled or mashed potatoes.

SERVES 4–6

900 g/2 lb stewing beef, such as
    chuck or leg
2 onions, thinly sliced
2 carrots, thickly sliced
4 large garlic cloves, bruised but kept
    whole
1 large fresh bouquet garni
4 juniper berries

500 ml/18 fl oz full-bodied dry red
    wine, such as Fitou
2 tbsp brandy
2 tbsp olive oil
225 g/8 oz boned belly of pork,
    rind removed
200 g/7 oz plain flour
2 x 10-cm/4-inch strips of orange rind

85 g/3 oz black olives, stoned and
    rinsed
beef stock, if needed
6 tbsp water
salt and pepper
1 tbsp chopped fresh flat-leaf parsley
    and finely grated orange rind,
    to garnish

Beef Stew with Olives

This traditional Provençal dish is often served with buttered noodles, but a mound of hot mashed potatoes also makes an ideal accompaniment. For a two-course meal in a pot Provençal-style, serve the flavoursome juices in a soup bowl with the noodles as a first course, then the meat and vegetables as a second course. You could also substitute 125 g/4½ oz unsmoked lardons for the belly of pork.

• Trim the beef and cut it into 5-cm/2-inch chunks, then put it in a large glass or earthenware bowl and add the onions, carrots, garlic, bouquet garni, juniper berries and salt and pepper to taste. Pour over the wine, brandy and oil and stir well. Cover with clingfilm and leave to marinate in the refrigerator for 24 hours.

• Remove the beef and marinade from the refrigerator 30 minutes before you plan to cook and preheat the oven to 160°C/325°F/Gas Mark 3. Meanwhile, cut the belly of pork into 5-mm/¼-inch strips. Bring a saucepan of water to the boil and add the pork. Return to the boil and blanch for 3 minutes, then drain and set aside.

• Using a slotted spoon, remove the beef from the marinade and pat dry with kitchen paper. Put the beef and 3 tablespoons of the flour, with salt and pepper to taste, in a polythene bag, hold the top closed and shake until the beef chunks are lightly coated all over. Remove the beef from the bag, shake off any excess flour and set aside.

• Transfer half the pork slices to a 3.4-litre/6-pint flameproof casserole. Top with the beef and marinade, including the vegetables and bouquet garni, and add the orange rind and olives. Scatter the remaining pork slices over. Top up with stock to cover all the ingredients.

• Mix the remaining flour with the water to form a thick, pliable paste. Slowly bring the casserole to the boil on the hob, then put the lid on the casserole and use your fingers to press the paste around the sides to form a tight seal. Cook in the preheated oven for 1 hour. Reduce the oven temperature to 140°C/275°F/Gas Mark 1 and cook for a further 3 hours.

• Remove the casserole from the oven and use a serrated knife to cut off the seal. Use the tip of the knife to ensure that the beef and carrots are tender. If not, re-cover the casserole and return it to the oven, testing again after 15 minutes.

• Using a large metal spoon, skim any fat from the surface and adjust the seasoning if necessary. Remove the bouquet garni, sprinkle the parsley and orange rind over the top and serve. Alternatively, leave to cool completely, cover and chill overnight. Before reheating, scrape the solid fat off the surface, reheat, garnish and serve.

SERVES 4–6

85 g/3 oz butter

2 tbsp sunflower oil

175 g/6 oz smoked lardons, blanched
for 30 seconds, drained and patted
dry

900 g/2 lb stewing beef, such as
chuck or leg

2 large garlic cloves, crushed

1 carrot, diced

1 leek, halved and sliced

1 onion, finely chopped

2 tbsp plain flour

350 ml/12 fl oz full-bodied red
Burgundy wine, such as Hermitage
or Côtes du Rhône

about 500 ml/18 fl oz beef stock

1 tbsp tomato purée

1 fresh bouquet garni

12 pickling onions, peeled but kept
whole

12 button mushrooms

salt and pepper

chopped fresh flat-leaf parsley,
to garnish

French bread, to serve

Beef Bourguignon

This casserole is customarily served with the same wine used in cooking. Like most meat casseroles, it tastes best made a day in advance and reheated. Remove from the oven after 1½ hours' simmering. The next day, cook the mushrooms and onions, add to the casserole and slowly bring to the boil on the hob, then cook in the preheated oven for 35–40 minutes until the beef is very tender.

- Preheat the oven to 150°C/300°F/Gas Mark 2. Heat 25 g/1 oz of the butter and 1 tablespoon of the oil in a large, flameproof casserole. Cook the lardons over a medium–high heat, stirring, for 2 minutes, or until beginning to brown. Using a slotted spoon, remove from the casserole and drain on kitchen paper.
- Trim the beef and cut it into 5-cm/2-inch chunks. Add the beef to the casserole and cook over a high heat, stirring frequently, for 5 minutes, or until browned on all sides and sealed, adding more of the butter or oil to the casserole as necessary. Using a slotted spoon, transfer the beef to a plate.
- Pour off all but 2 tablespoons of the fat from the casserole. Add the garlic, carrot, leek and chopped onion and cook over a medium heat, stirring frequently, for 3 minutes, or until the onion is beginning to soften. Sprinkle in the flour, and salt and pepper to taste, and cook, stirring constantly, for 2 minutes, then remove the casserole from the heat.
- Gradually stir in the wine and stock and add the tomato purée and bouquet garni, then return to the heat and bring to the boil, stirring and scraping any sediment from the base of the casserole.
- Return the beef and lardons to the casserole and add extra stock if necessary so that the ingredients are covered by about 1 cm/½ inch of liquid. Slowly return to the boil, then cover and cook in the preheated oven for 2 hours. Meanwhile, heat 25 g/1 oz of the remaining butter and the remaining oil in a large sauté pan or frying pan and cook the pickling onions over a medium–high heat, stirring frequently, until golden all over. Using a slotted spoon, transfer the onions to a plate.
- Heat the remaining butter in the pan and cook the mushrooms, with salt and pepper to taste, stirring frequently, until golden brown. Remove from the pan and then stir them, with the onions, into the casserole, re-cover and cook for a further 30 minutes, or until the beef is very tender.
- Discard the bouquet garni, then adjust the seasoning to taste. Serve garnished with parsley, accompanied by plenty of French bread for mopping up all the juices.

SERVES 4

450 g/1 lb lean boneless lamb, such
    as leg of lamb or fillet
1½ tbsp plain flour
1 tsp ground cloves
1–1½ tbsp olive oil
1 white onion, sliced
2–3 garlic cloves, sliced

300 ml/10 fl oz orange juice
150 ml/5 fl oz lamb stock or chicken
    stock
1 cinnamon stick, bruised
2 sweet (pointed, if available) red
    peppers, deseeded and sliced into
    rings
4 tomatoes

few fresh sprigs coriander, plus
    1 tbsp chopped fresh coriander,
    to garnish
salt and pepper
mashed sweet potatoes mixed with
    chopped spring onions, to serve
green vegetables, to serve

Lamb Stew with Sweet Red Peppers

Sweet potatoes are very good for mashing and offer a tasty alternative to the traditional potato as an accompaniment. Try combining sweet potatoes with parsnips or carrot and mash together, then stir in a little chopped fresh coriander.

• Preheat the oven to 190°C/375°F/Gas Mark 5. Trim any fat or gristle from the lamb and cut into thin strips. Mix the flour and cloves together. Toss the lamb in the spiced flour until well coated and reserve any remaining spiced flour.

• Heat 1 tablespoon of the oil in a heavy-based frying pan and cook the lamb over a high heat, stirring frequently, for 3 minutes, or until browned on all sides and sealed. Using a slotted spoon, transfer to an ovenproof casserole.

• Add the onion and garlic to the frying pan and cook over a medium heat, stirring frequently, for 3 minutes, adding the extra oil if necessary. Sprinkle in the reserved spiced flour and cook, stirring constantly, for 2 minutes, then remove from the heat. Gradually stir in the orange juice and stock, then return to the heat and bring to the boil, stirring.

• Pour over the lamb in the casserole, add the cinnamon stick, red peppers, tomatoes and coriander sprigs and stir well. Cover and cook in the preheated oven for 1½ hours, or until the lamb is tender.

• Discard the cinnamon stick, and adjust the seasoning to taste. Serve garnished with the chopped coriander, accompanied by mashed sweet potatoes with spring onions, and green vegetables.

SERVES 6

2 tbsp plain flour

1 kg/2 lb 4 oz lean boneless lamb, cubed

2 tbsp olive oil

2 large onions, sliced

1 garlic clove, finely chopped

300 ml/10 fl oz full-bodied red wine

2 tbsp red wine vinegar

400 g/14 oz canned chopped tomatoes

55 g/2 oz seedless raisins

1 tbsp ground cinnamon

pinch of sugar

1 bay leaf

salt and pepper

paprika, to garnish

TOPPING

150 ml/5 fl oz authentic natural Greek yogurt

2 garlic cloves, crushed

salt and pepper

Cinnamon Lamb Casserole

Serve this dish with potatoes, rice or a pilaf to soak up the delicious aromatic juices.

• Season the flour with pepper to taste then put it with the lamb in a polythene bag, hold the top closed and shake until the lamb cubes are lightly coated all over. Remove the lamb from the bag, shake off any excess flour and set aside.

• Heat the oil in a large, flameproof casserole and cook the onions and garlic, stirring frequently, for 5 minutes, or until softened. Add the lamb and cook over a high heat, stirring frequently, for 5 minutes, or until browned on all sides and sealed.

• Stir the wine, vinegar and tomatoes and their can juices into the casserole, scraping any sediment from the base of the casserole, and bring to the boil. Reduce the heat and add the raisins, cinnamon, sugar and bay leaf. Season to taste with salt and pepper. Cover and simmer gently for 2 hours, or until the lamb is tender.

• Meanwhile, make the topping. Put the yogurt into a small serving bowl, stir in the garlic and season to taste with salt and pepper. Cover and chill in the refrigerator until required.

• Discard the bay leaf and serve hot, topped with a spoonful of the garlicky yogurt and dusted with paprika.

SERVES 4

pinch of saffron threads

2 tbsp almost boiling water

450 g/1 lb lean boneless lamb,
    such as leg steaks

1½ tbsp plain flour

1 tsp ground coriander

½ tsp ground cumin

½ tsp ground allspice

1 tbsp olive oil

1 onion, chopped

2–3 garlic cloves, chopped

450 ml/16 fl oz lamb or chicken stock

1 cinnamon stick, bruised

85 g/3 oz dried apricots, roughly
    chopped

175 g/6 oz courgettes, sliced

115 g/4 oz cherry tomatoes

1 tbsp chopped fresh coriander

salt and pepper

2 tbsp roughly chopped pistachio
    nuts, to garnish

couscous, to serve

Mediterranean Lamb with Apricots & Pistachio Nuts

Couscous is now available in an instant form, which is simply prepared by pouring over boiling water, then quickly stirring, covering and leaving for 5–8 minutes. Fluff up with a fork before serving. Alternatively, scatter a handful of raisins over the couscous and use boiling lamb, chicken or vegetable stock in place of the water.

• Put the saffron threads in a heatproof jug with the water and leave for at least 10 minutes to infuse. Trim off any fat or gristle from the lamb and cut into 2.5-cm/1-inch chunks. Mix the flour and spices together, then toss the lamb in the spiced flour until well coated and reserve any remaining spiced flour.

• Heat the oil in a large, heavy-based saucepan and cook the onion and garlic, stirring frequently, for 5 minutes, or until softened. Add the lamb and cook over a high heat, stirring frequently, for 3 minutes, or until browned on all sides and sealed. Sprinkle in the reserved spiced flour and cook, stirring constantly, for 2 minutes, then remove from the heat.

• Gradually stir in the stock and the saffron and its soaking liquid, then return to the heat and bring to the boil, stirring. Add the cinnamon stick and apricots. Reduce the heat, cover and simmer, stirring occasionally, for 1 hour. Add the courgettes and tomatoes and cook for a further 15 minutes. Discard the cinnamon stick. Stir in the fresh coriander and season to taste with salt and pepper. Serve sprinkled with the pistachio nuts, accompanied by couscous.

SERVES 4

450 g/1 lb lean boneless pork

1½ tbsp plain flour

1–2 tbsp olive oil

1 onion, cut into small wedges

2–3 garlic cloves, chopped

2.5-cm/1-inch piece fresh root ginger, peeled and grated

1 tbsp tomato purée

300 ml/10 fl oz chicken stock

225 g/8 oz canned pineapple chunks in natural juice

1–1½ tbsp dark soy sauce

1 red pepper, deseeded and sliced

1 green pepper, deseeded and sliced

1½ tbsp balsamic vinegar

4 spring onions, diagonally sliced, to garnish

Pork Oriental

This dish also works well with chicken, turkey or gammon. Serve it with freshly cooked rice – stir in a little chopped fresh coriander just before serving.

• Trim off any fat or gristle from the pork and cut into 2.5-cm/1-inch chunks. Toss the pork in the flour until well coated and reserve any remaining flour.

• Heat the oil in a large, heavy-based saucepan and cook the onion, garlic and ginger, stirring frequently, for 5 minutes, or until softened. Add the pork and cook over a high heat, stirring frequently, for 5 minutes, or until browned on all sides and sealed. Sprinkle in the reserved flour and cook, stirring constantly, for 2 minutes, then remove from the heat.

• Blend the tomato purée with the stock in a heatproof jug and gradually stir into the saucepan. Drain the pineapple, reserving both the fruit and juice, and stir the juice into the saucepan.

• Add the soy sauce to the saucepan, then return to the heat and bring to the boil, stirring. Reduce the heat, cover and simmer, stirring occasionally, for 1 hour. Add the peppers and cook for a further 15 minutes, or until the pork is tender. Stir in the vinegar and the pineapple fruit and heat through for 5 minutes. Serve sprinkled with the spring onions.

SERVES 4

450 g/1 lb lean boneless pork

1½ tbsp plain flour

1 tsp ground coriander

1 tsp ground cumin

1½ tsp ground cinnamon

1 tbsp olive oil

1 onion, chopped

400 g/14 oz canned chopped
   tomatoes

2 tbsp tomato purée

300–450 ml/10–16 fl oz chicken stock

225 g/8 oz carrots, chopped

350 g/12 oz squash, such as kabocha,
   peeled, deseeded and chopped

225 g/8 oz leeks, sliced, blanched and
   drained

115 g/4 oz okra, trimmed and sliced

salt and pepper

sprigs of fresh parsley, to garnish

couscous, to serve

Pork & Vegetable Ragout

The squash used in this recipe is sometimes quite difficult to find. If that's the case, substitute either acorn or butternut squash.

• Trim off any fat or gristle from the pork and cut into thin strips about 5 cm/2 inches long. Mix the flour and spices together. Toss the pork in the spiced flour until well coated and reserve any remaining spiced flour. Heat the oil in a large, heavy-based saucepan and cook the onion, stirring frequently, for 5 minutes, or until softened. Add the pork and cook over a high heat, stirring frequently, for 5 minutes, or until browned on all sides and sealed. Sprinkle in the reserved spiced flour and cook, stirring constantly, for 2 minutes, then remove from the heat.

• Gradually stir the tomatoes into the saucepan. Blend the tomato purée with a little of the stock in a jug and gradually stir into the saucepan, then stir in half the remaining stock.

• Add the carrots, then return to the heat and bring to the boil, stirring. Reduce the heat, cover and simmer, stirring occasionally, for 1½ hours. Add the squash and cook for a further 15 minutes.

• Add the leeks and okra, and the remaining stock if you prefer a thinner ragout. Simmer for a further 15 minutes, or until the pork and vegetables are tender. Season to taste with salt and pepper, then garnish with fresh parsley and serve with couscous.

SERVES 4

450–550 g/1–1 lb 4 oz lean gammon

1–2 tbsp olive oil, plus 1–2 tsp

1 onion, chopped

2–3 garlic cloves, chopped

2 celery sticks, chopped

175 g/6 oz sliced carrots

1 cinnamon stick, bruised

½ tsp ground cloves

¼ tsp freshly grated nutmeg

1 tsp dried oregano, plus 1 tbsp
    chopped fresh oregano to garnish

450 ml/16 fl oz chicken stock or
    vegetable stock

1–2 tbsp maple syrup

3 large, spicy sausages, about
    225 g/8 oz, or chorizo (outer casing
    removed)

400 g/14 oz canned black-eyed beans
    or broad beans

1 orange pepper

1 tbsp cornflour

pepper

creamed mashed potatoes, to serve

Gammon with Black-eyed Beans

In order to get the maximum flavour from a cinnamon stick, it is a good idea to bruise it lightly. Simply crush the cinnamon stick in your hands very gently without breaking it up altogether. This really does help to release the delicate taste.

• Trim off any fat or skin from the gammon and cut into 4-cm/1½-inch chunks. Heat 1 tablespoon of oil in a heavy-based saucepan and cook the gammon over a high heat, stirring frequently, for 5 minutes, or until browned on all sides and sealed. Using a slotted spoon, remove from the saucepan and set aside.
• Add the onion, garlic, celery and carrots to the saucepan with a further 1 tablespoon of oil if necessary and cook over a medium heat, stirring frequently, for 5 minutes, or until softened. Add all the spices, season with pepper to taste, and cook, stirring constantly, for 2 minutes.
• Return the gammon to the saucepan. Add the dried oregano, stock, and maple syrup to taste, then bring to the boil, stirring. Reduce the heat, cover and simmer, stirring occasionally, for 1 hour.
• Heat the remaining 1–2 teaspoons of oil in a frying pan and cook the sausages, turning frequently, until browned all over. Remove and cut each into 3–4 chunks, then add to the saucepan. Drain and rinse the beans, then drain again. Deseed and chop the orange pepper. Add the beans and pepper to the pan, and simmer for a further 20 minutes. Blend 2 tablespoons of water with the cornflour and stir into the stew, then cook for 3–5 minutes. Discard the cinnamon stick. Serve garnished with fresh oregano, accompanied by creamed mashed potatoes.

Poultry, and chicken in particular, is a sure-fire winner, because it always tastes good and is universally popular with even the most cautious of meat eaters, including children. Its easy-going texture makes it easy to digest, and it is lean and healthy, especially when the skin is removed. When it comes to stews and casseroles, it is also highly versatile, since chicken portions, a whole chicken divided into pieces, or chunks of chicken can be used. Chicken portions with bones obviously take longer to cook than boneless chunks, but the cooking time is still far less than for meat, so it is ideal for when a shorter cooking time is required. But whenever cooking whole portions of chicken, always ensure that they are thoroughly cooked by inserting a skewer into the thickest part of the meat and checking that the juices are clear. If they are pink, further cooking is needed.

POULTRY & GAME

Game offers an extra dimension in stews and casseroles, with its more complex, fulsome taste and robust texture producing a rich, sophisticated result. Here we feature pheasant and duck as well as venison.

Again, flavours are drawn from around the globe in these recipes. Rich and creamy Chicken in Riesling is Alsace's answer to Coq au Vin, while Florida Chicken speaks for itself, its name referring to the fresh orange flesh and juice, which complement the delicate taste of chicken so well. On the game side, duck is the main ingredient of a Creole classic, Duck Jambalaya-style Stew, along with its traditional additions of gammon, tomatoes, green pepper and rice, all spiked with chilli.

SERVES 4

4 chicken portions, about
    150 g/5½ oz each
1½ tbsp plain flour
2 tbsp olive oil
1 onion, chopped
2–3 garlic cloves, chopped
1 fresh red chilli, deseeded and
    chopped

225 g/8 oz chorizo, outer casing
    removed, or spicy sausages,
    cut into small chunks
300 ml/10 fl oz chicken stock
150 ml/5 fl oz white wine or additional
    chicken stock
1 tbsp dark soy sauce
1 large red pepper, deseeded and
    sliced into rings

225 g/8 oz frozen or shelled fresh
    broad beans, thawed if frozen
25 g/1 oz rocket or baby spinach
    leaves
salt and pepper
long-grain rice, to serve

Chicken with Red Pepper & Broad Beans

If using frozen broad beans in this dish, thawing them beforehand is a good idea, as adding frozen beans to the casserole will lower the temperature of the dish and the chicken could take longer to cook.

• Preheat the oven to 190°C/375°F/Gas Mark 5. Lightly rinse the chicken and pat dry with kitchen paper. Season the flour well with salt and pepper. Toss the chicken in the seasoned flour until well coated and reserve any remaining seasoned flour.

• Heat half the oil in a large, heavy-based frying pan and cook the chicken over a medium–high heat, turning frequently, for 10 minutes, or until golden all over and sealed, adding more of the remaining oil if necessary. Using a slotted spoon, transfer to an ovenproof casserole.

• Add the remaining oil to the frying pan and cook the onion, garlic and chilli over a medium heat, stirring frequently, for 5 minutes, or until softened. Add the chorizo and cook, stirring frequently, for 2 minutes. Sprinkle in the reserved seasoned flour and cook, stirring constantly, for 2 minutes, then remove from the heat. Gradually stir in the stock, wine and soy sauce, then return to the heat and bring to the boil, stirring.

• Pour over the chicken in the casserole, cover and cook in the preheated oven for 25 minutes. Add the red pepper and cook for a further 10 minutes. Add the broad beans and cook for a further 10 minutes, or until the chicken and vegetables are tender and the chicken juices run clear when a skewer is inserted into the thickest part of the meat.

• Remove from the oven. Taste and adjust the seasoning, then stir in the rocket and leave for 2 minutes, or until wilted. Serve with rice.

SERVES 4

15 g/½ oz unsalted butter

2 tbsp olive oil

1.8 kg/4 lb skinned, unboned chicken
    portions

2 red onions, sliced

2 garlic cloves, finely chopped

400 g/14 oz canned chopped
    tomatoes

2 tbsp chopped fresh flat-leaf parsley

6 fresh basil leaves, torn

1 tbsp sun-dried tomato paste

150 ml/5 fl oz red wine

225 g/8 oz mushrooms, sliced

salt and pepper

Hunter's Chicken

Try substituting Marsala for
the red wine, and adding
1 deseeded and sliced
green pepper with
the onions.

• Preheat the oven to 160°C/325°F/Gas Mark 3. Heat the butter and oil in a flameproof casserole and cook the chicken over a medium–high heat, turning frequently, for 10 minutes, or until golden all over and sealed. Using a slotted spoon, transfer to a plate.

• Add the onions and garlic to the casserole and cook over a low heat, stirring occasionally, for 10 minutes, or until softened and golden. Add the tomatoes with their juice, the herbs, sun-dried tomato paste and wine, and season to taste with salt and pepper. Bring to the boil, then return the chicken portions to the casserole, pushing them down into the sauce.

• Cover and cook in the preheated oven for 50 minutes. Add the mushrooms and cook for a further 10 minutes, or until the chicken is tender and the juices run clear when a skewer is inserted into the thickest part of the meat. Serve immediately.

SERVES 4

4 chicken portions, about
   150 g/5½ oz each
1 tbsp plain flour
2½ tbsp olive oil
8–12 shallots, halved if large

2–4 garlic cloves, sliced
400 ml/14 fl oz chicken stock
50 ml/2 fl oz sherry
few sprigs fresh thyme, plus 1 tbsp
   chopped fresh thyme to garnish
115 g/4 oz cherry tomatoes

115 g/4 oz baby sweetcorn, halved
   lengthways
2 large slices white or wholemeal
   bread
salt and pepper

Poulet Marengo-Style

After frying and while still hot, you can toss the croutons in finely chopped fresh thyme or finely grated Parmesan cheese for additional flavour.

• Lightly rinse the chicken and pat dry with kitchen paper. Season the flour well with salt and pepper. Toss the chicken in the seasoned flour until well coated and reserve any remaining seasoned flour.

• Heat 1 tablespoon of the oil in a large, deep frying pan and cook the chicken over a medium–high heat, turning frequently, for 10 minutes, or until golden all over and sealed. Using a slotted spoon, transfer to a plate.

• Add the shallots and garlic to the frying pan and cook over a medium heat, stirring frequently, for 5 minutes, or until softened. Sprinkle in the reserved seasoned flour and cook, stirring constantly, for 2 minutes, then remove from the heat. Gradually stir in the stock followed by the sherry, then return to the heat and bring to the boil, stirring.

• Return the chicken to the frying pan and add the thyme sprigs. Reduce the heat, cover and simmer, stirring occasionally, for 40 minutes. Add the tomatoes and baby sweetcorn and simmer for a further 10 minutes, or until the chicken is tender and the juices run clear when a skewer is inserted into the thickest part of the meat.

• Meanwhile, cut the bread into small cubes. Heat the remaining oil in a frying pan and fry the bread, stirring frequently, for 4–5 minutes, or until golden. Serve the stew garnished with the chopped thyme and the croûtons.

SERVES 6

1.8 kg/4 lb chicken portions

2 tbsp paprika

2 tbsp olive oil

25 g/1 oz butter

450 g/1 lb onions

2 yellow peppers

400 g/14 oz canned chopped
    tomatoes

225 ml/8 fl oz dry white wine

450 ml/16 fl oz chicken stock

1 tbsp Worcestershire sauce

½ tsp Tabasco sauce

1 tbsp finely chopped fresh parsley

325 g/11½ oz canned sweetcorn
    kernels, drained

425 g/15 oz canned butter beans,
    drained and rinsed

2 tbsp plain flour

4 tbsp water

salt

fresh sprigs of parsley, to garnish

Brunswick Stew

If you decide to substitute fresh tomatoes for canned tomatoes in a stew, add 1 tablespoon of tomato purée to the dish at the same time, to make sure that the flavour is strong enough.

• Season the chicken to taste with salt, and dust with the paprika.
• Heat the oil and butter in a flameproof casserole or large saucepan and cook the chicken over a medium–high heat, turning frequently, for 10 minutes, or until golden all over and sealed. Using a slotted spoon, transfer to a plate.
• Chop the onions and deseed and chop the yellow peppers then add them to the casserole and cook over a medium heat, stirring frequently, for 5 minutes, or until softened. Add the tomatoes, wine, stock, Worcestershire sauce, Tabasco sauce and parsley and bring to the boil, stirring. Return the chicken to the casserole, cover and simmer, stirring occasionally, for 30 minutes.
• Add the sweetcorn and butter beans to the casserole, partially re-cover and simmer for a further 30 minutes. Put the flour and water in a small bowl and blend to make a paste. Stir a ladleful of the cooking liquid into the paste, then stir it into the stew. Cook, stirring frequently, for 5 minutes, or until thickened. Serve garnished with parsley sprigs.

SERVES 4

4 chicken portions,
    about 150 g/5½ oz each,
    skinned if preferred
1 tbsp olive oil
1 onion, chopped
2 celery sticks, roughly chopped
1½ tbsp plain flour

300 ml/10 fl oz clear apple juice
150 ml/5 fl oz chicken stock
1 cooking apple, cored and quartered
2 bay leaves
1–2 tsp clear honey
1 yellow pepper, deseeded and cut
    into chunks
1 tbsp butter

1 large or 2 medium eating apples,
    cored and sliced
2 tbsp demerara sugar
salt and pepper
1 tbsp chopped fresh mint, to garnish

Chicken & Apple Pot

You could add a couple of tablespoons of Calvados – a dry apple brandy from Normandy in France – to intensify the apple flavours in this dish.

- Preheat the oven to 190°C/375°F/Gas Mark 5. Lightly rinse the chicken and pat dry with kitchen paper. Heat the oil in a deep frying pan and cook the chicken over a medium–high heat, turning frequently, for 10 minutes, or until golden all over and sealed. Using a slotted spoon, transfer to an ovenproof casserole.
- Add the onion and celery to the frying pan and cook over a medium heat, stirring frequently, for 5 minutes, or until softened. Sprinkle in the flour and cook, stirring constantly, for 2 minutes, then remove from the heat.
- Gradually stir in the apple juice and stock, then return to the heat and bring to the boil, stirring. Add the cooking apple, bay leaves, and honey and season to taste.
- Pour over the chicken in the casserole, cover and cook in the preheated oven for 25 minutes. Add the yellow pepper and cook for a further 10–15 minutes, or until the chicken is tender and the juices run clear when a skewer is inserted into the thickest part of the meat.
- Meanwhile, preheat the grill to high. Melt the butter in a saucepan over a low heat. Line the grill pan with kitchen foil. Brush the eating apple slices with half the butter, sprinkle with a little sugar and cook under the grill for 2–3 minutes, or until the sugar has caramelized. Turn the slices over, brush with the remaining butter and sprinkle with the remaining sugar, then cook for a further 2 minutes. Serve the stew garnished with the mint and caramelized apple slices.

SERVES 4–6

1 chicken, weighing
   1.6 kg/3 lb 8 oz, cut into
   8 pieces, or 8 chicken thighs
2 tbsp plain flour
55 g/2 oz unsalted butter

1 tbsp sunflower oil
4 shallots, finely chopped
12 button mushrooms, sliced
2 tbsp brandy
500 ml/18 fl oz Riesling wine
250 ml/9 fl oz double cream

salt and pepper
chopped fresh flat-leaf parsley,
   to garnish

Chicken in Riesling

Take great care when igniting the brandy and use a long-handled match. Set light to the fumes rather than the actual brandy.

• Put the chicken and flour, with salt and pepper to taste, in a polythene bag, hold the top closed and shake until the chicken pieces are lightly coated all over. Remove the chicken from the bag, shake off any excess flour and set aside.

• Heat 25 g/1 oz of the butter and all of the oil in a large sauté pan or frying pan with a tight-fitting lid, or a flameproof casserole, and cook the chicken over a medium–high heat, turning frequently, for 10 minutes, or until golden all over and sealed. Using a slotted spoon, transfer to a plate.

• Pour off all the fat in the pan and wipe the pan with kitchen paper. Heat the remaining butter in the pan over a medium–high heat. When the butter stops foaming, cook the shallots and mushrooms, stirring constantly, for 3 minutes, or until the shallots are golden and the mushrooms are lightly browned.

• Return the chicken to the pan and remove the pan from the heat. Warm the brandy in a ladle or small saucepan, ignite and pour it over the chicken to flambé.

• When the flames die down, return the pan to the heat, pour in the wine and slowly bring to the boil, scraping any sediment from the base of the pan. Reduce the heat to low, cover and simmer for 40–45 minutes, until the chicken is tender and the juices run clear when a skewer is inserted into the thickest part of the meat.

• Meanwhile, preheat the oven to its lowest temperature. Using a slotted spoon, transfer the chicken to a large serving platter and keep it warm in the oven.

• Tilt the pan and use a large metal spoon to remove the fat from the surface of the cooking liquid. Stir in the cream and bring the sauce to the boil. The sauce will boil quickly and should reduce by half almost instantly. Add salt and pepper to taste.

• To serve, spoon the sauce with the mushrooms and shallots over the chicken and sprinkle with the parsley to garnish.

SERVES 4

450 g/1 lb skinless, boneless chicken

1½ tbsp plain flour

1 tbsp olive oil

1 onion, cut into wedges

2 celery sticks, sliced

150 ml/5 fl oz orange juice

300 ml/10 fl oz chicken stock

1 tbsp light soy sauce

1–2 tsp clear honey

1 tbsp grated orange rind

1 orange pepper, deseeded and
    chopped

225 g/8 oz courgettes, sliced into half
    moons

2 small corn on the cobs, halved, or
    100 g/3½ oz baby sweetcorn

1 orange, peeled and segmented

salt and pepper

1 tbsp chopped fresh parsley,
    to garnish

Florida Chicken

Instead of using honey, try maple syrup (provided it is the real thing) to add an extra dimension to the flavour.

• Lightly rinse the chicken and pat dry with kitchen paper. Cut into bite-sized pieces. Season the flour well with salt and pepper. Toss the chicken in the seasoned flour until well coated and reserve any remaining seasoned flour.

• Heat the oil in a large, heavy-based frying pan and cook the chicken over a high heat, stirring frequently, for 5 minutes, or until golden on all sides and sealed. Using a slotted spoon, transfer to a plate.

• Add the onion and celery to the frying pan and cook over a medium heat, stirring frequently, for 5 minutes, or until softened. Sprinkle in the reserved seasoned flour and cook, stirring constantly, for 2 minutes, then remove from the heat. Gradually stir in the orange juice, stock, soy sauce and honey followed by the orange rind, then return to the heat and bring to the boil, stirring.

• Return the chicken to the frying pan. Reduce the heat, cover and simmer, stirring occasionally, for 15 minutes. Add the orange pepper, courgettes and corn on the cob and simmer for a further 10 minutes, or until the chicken and vegetables are tender. Add the orange segments, stir well and heat through for 1 minute. Serve garnished with the parsley.

SERVES 4

4 duck portions, about
150 g/5½ oz each

1–2 tsp olive oil, plus 1 tbsp (optional)

1 red onion, cut into wedges

2–3 garlic cloves, chopped

1 large carrot, chopped

2 celery sticks, chopped

2 tbsp plain flour

300 ml/10 fl oz red wine,
such as Claret

2 tbsp brandy (optional)

150–200 ml/5–7 fl oz stock or water

7.5-cm/3-inch strip of orange rind

2 tsp redcurrant jelly

115 g/4 oz sugarsnap peas

115 g/4 oz button mushrooms

salt and pepper

1 tbsp chopped fresh parsley,
to garnish

Duck & Red Wine Stew

If using duck breasts only, the cooking time can be reduced by about 15 minutes.

• Remove and discard the fat from the duck. Lightly rinse and pat dry with kitchen paper.

• Heat a large, deep frying pan for 1 minute until warm but not piping hot. Put the duck portions in the frying pan and gently heat until the fat starts to run. Increase the heat a little, then cook, turning over halfway through, for 5 minutes, or until browned on both sides and sealed. Using a slotted spoon, transfer to a flameproof casserole.

• Add 1 tablespoon of the oil if there is little duck fat in the frying pan and cook the onion, garlic, carrot and celery, stirring frequently, for 5 minutes, or until softened. Sprinkle in the flour and cook, stirring constantly, for 2 minutes, then remove the frying pan from the heat.

• Gradually stir in the wine, brandy (if using), and stock, then return to the heat and bring to the boil, stirring. Season to taste with salt and pepper, then add the orange rind and redcurrant jelly. Pour over the duck portions in the casserole, cover and simmer, stirring occasionally, for 1–1¼ hours.

• Cook the sugarsnap peas in a saucepan of boiling water for 3 minutes, then drain and add to the stew. Meanwhile, heat 1–2 teaspoons of the olive oil in a small saucepan and cook the mushrooms, stirring frequently, for 3 minutes, or until beginning to soften. Add to the stew. Cook the stew for a further 5 minutes, or until the duck is tender. Serve garnished with the parsley.

SERVES 4

4 duck breasts, about
   150 g/5½ oz each
2 tbsp olive oil
225 g/8 oz piece gammon,
   cut into small chunks
225 g/8 oz chorizo, outer casing
   removed
1 onion, chopped

3 garlic cloves, chopped
3 celery sticks, chopped
1–2 fresh red chillies, deseeded and
   chopped
1 green pepper, deseeded and
   chopped
600 ml/1 pint chicken stock
1 tbsp chopped fresh oregano

400 g/14 oz canned chopped
   tomatoes
1–2 tsp hot pepper sauce, or to taste
salt
fresh sprigs of parsley, to garnish
green salad and long-grain rice,
   to serve

Duck Jambalaya-style Stew

This is a great dish to serve at an informal supper party, with plenty of salad and crusty bread. Use a large deep dish for serving it and put the rice in first, then spoon over the Jambalaya. Serve with chilled lager or white wine.

• Remove and discard the skin and any fat from the duck breasts. Cut the flesh into bite-sized pieces.
• Heat half the oil in a large deep frying pan and cook the duck, gammon and chorizo over a high heat, stirring frequently, for 5 minutes, or until browned on all sides and sealed. Using a slotted spoon, remove from the frying pan and set aside.
• Add the onion, garlic, celery and chilli to the frying pan and cook over a medium heat, stirring frequently, for 5 minutes, or until softened. Add the green pepper, then stir in the stock, oregano, tomatoes and hot pepper sauce.
• Bring to the boil, then reduce the heat and return the duck, gammon and chorizo to the frying pan. Cover and simmer, stirring occasionally, for 20 minutes, or until the duck and gammon are tender. Serve accompanied by a green salad and rice.

It may seem surprising to some people to feature fish and shellfish in stews and casseroles, but in fact there are many traditional stew recipes originating from around the Mediterranean that consist largely of fish, with vegetables playing a supporting role. This is not so surprising really when you consider the abundance of seafood and array of colourful, sun-ripened vegetables that the region has to offer. In addition to the classic Mediterranean dishes, this chapter includes recipes from the East, with their characteristically aromatic flavours, along with a piquant taste of Creole cooking from Louisiana.

When cooking fish and shellfish stews and casseroles, it is best to prepare all the ingredients before starting to cook the dish, since these star items take a short time and their flavour and texture will be easily impaired if overcooked. Also, these dishes should be

SIMMERING SEAFOOD

eaten as soon as they have been cooked, and not reheated. If using frozen fish, it is worth thawing the fish slowly, leaving it on a large plate, lightly covered, in the refrigerator overnight. The next day, rinse lightly, pat dry with kitchen paper, then return to the refrigerator until required.

Many of these dishes contain prawns. Instructions on how to peel and devein prawns are given on page 140, and contrary to popular belief this is not a difficult process! Ensure that you wash the prawns well before you begin to cook them.

SERVES 9

1.25 kg/2 lb 12 oz sea bass, filleted,
    skinned and cut into bite-sized
    chunks
1.25 kg/2 lb 12 oz redfish, filleted,
    skinned and cut into bite-sized
    chunks
3 tbsp extra virgin olive oil
grated rind of 1 orange

1 garlic clove, finely chopped
pinch of saffron threads
2 tbsp pastis, such as Pernod
450 g/1 lb live mussels
1 large cooked crab
1 small fennel bulb, finely chopped
2 celery sticks, finely chopped
1 onion, finely chopped
1.2 litres/2 pints fish stock

225 g/8 oz small new potatoes,
    scrubbed
225 g/8 oz tomatoes, peeled,
    deseeded and chopped
450 g/1 lb large raw prawns,
    peeled and deveined
salt and pepper

Bouillabaisse

Redfish, or Norwegian haddock, is related to the scorpion fish. It is a traditional ingredient in bouillabaisse, but if you cannot find it, use red mullet instead.

• Put the fish pieces in a large bowl and add 2 tablespoons of the oil, the orange rind, garlic, saffron and pastis. Toss the fish pieces until well coated, cover and leave to marinate in the refrigerator for 30 minutes.
• Meanwhile, clean the mussels by scrubbing or scraping the shells and pulling out any beards that are attached to them. Discard any with broken shells or any that refuse to close when tapped. Remove the meat from the crab, chop and reserve.
• Heat the remaining oil in a large, flameproof casserole and cook the fennel, celery and onion over a low heat, stirring occasionally, for 5 minutes, or until softened. Add the stock and bring to the boil. Add the potatoes and tomatoes and cook over a medium heat for 7 minutes.
• Reduce the heat and add the fish to the stew, beginning with the thickest pieces, then add the mussels, prawns and crab and simmer until the fish is opaque, the mussels have opened and the prawns have turned pink. Discard any mussels that remain closed. Season to taste with salt and pepper and serve immediately.

SERVES 4

1 yellow pepper, 1 red pepper,
    1 orange pepper, deseeded
    and quartered
450 g/1 lb ripe tomatoes
2 large, fresh, mild green chillies, such
    as poblano
6 garlic cloves, peeled but kept whole

2 tsp dried oregano or dried mixed
    herbs
2 tbsp olive oil, plus extra for drizzling
1 large onion, finely chopped
450 ml/16 fl oz fish stock, vegetable
    or chicken stock
finely grated rind and juice of 1 lime
2 tbsp chopped fresh coriander,
    plus extra to garnish

1 bay leaf
450 g/1 lb red snapper fillets, skinned
    and cut into chunks
225 g/8 oz raw prawns, peeled and
    deveined
225 g/8 oz raw squid rings
salt and pepper
warmed flour tortillas, to serve

South-western Seafood Stew

Roasting the peppers, tomatoes, chillies and garlic enhances the flavour of this sumptuous seafood medley. You can use any other firm fish fillets or a mixture, if you prefer.

• Preheat the oven to 200°C/400°F/Gas Mark 6. Put the pepper quarters, skin-side up, in a roasting tin with the tomatoes, chillies and garlic. Sprinkle with the oregano and drizzle with oil. Roast in the preheated oven for 30 minutes, or until the peppers are well browned and softened.

• Remove the roasted vegetables from the oven and leave to stand until cool enough to handle. Peel off the skins from the peppers, tomatoes and chillies and chop the flesh. Finely chop the garlic.

• Heat the oil in a large saucepan and cook the onion, stirring frequently, for 5 minutes, or until softened. Add the peppers, tomatoes, chillies, garlic, stock, lime rind and juice, coriander, bay leaf, and salt and pepper to taste. Bring to the boil, then stir in the seafood. Reduce the heat, cover and gently simmer for 10 minutes, or until the fish and squid is just cooked through and the prawns have turned pink. Discard the bay leaf, then garnish with chopped coriander before serving, accompanied by warmed flour tortillas.

SERVES 4–6

large pinch of saffron threads

4 tbsp almost boiling water

6 tbsp olive oil

1 large onion, chopped

2 garlic cloves, finely chopped

1½ tbsp chopped fresh thyme leaves

2 bay leaves

2 red peppers, deseeded and roughly chopped

800 g/1 lb 12 oz canned chopped tomatoes

1 tsp smoked paprika

250 ml/9 fl oz fish stock

140 g/5 oz blanched almonds, toasted and finely ground

12–16 live mussels

12–16 live clams

600 g/1 lb 5 oz thick boned hake or cod fillets, skinned and cut into 5-cm/2-inch chunks

12–16 raw prawns, peeled and deveined

salt and pepper

thick crusty bread, to serve

Catalan Fish Stew

Take care not to overcook the hake, or it will break into flakes that have very little texture. Monkfish is an excellent alternative to hake or cod.

• Put the saffron threads in a heatproof jug with the water and leave for at least 10 minutes to infuse.

• Heat the oil in a large, heavy-based flameproof casserole over a medium–high heat. Reduce the heat to low and cook the onion, stirring occasionally, for 10 minutes, or until golden but not browned. Stir in the garlic, thyme, bay leaves and red peppers and cook, stirring frequently, for 5 minutes, or until the peppers are softened and the onions have softened further.

• Add the tomatoes and paprika and simmer, stirring frequently, for a further 5 minutes. Stir in the stock, the saffron and its soaking liquid and the almonds and bring to the boil, stirring. Reduce the heat and simmer for 5–10 minutes, until the sauce reduces and thickens. Season to taste with salt and pepper.

• Meanwhile, clean the mussels and clams by scrubbing or scraping the shells and pulling out any beards that are attached to the mussels. Discard any with broken shells or any that refuse to close when tapped.

• Gently stir the hake into the stew so that it doesn't break up, then add the prawns, mussels and clams. Reduce the heat to very low, cover and simmer for 5 minutes, or until the hake is opaque, the mussels and clams have opened and the prawns have turned pink. Discard any mussels or clams that remain closed. Serve immediately with plenty of thick crusty bread for soaking up the juices.

SERVES 4–6

large pinch of saffron threads

900 g/2 lb fresh Mediterranean fish, such as sea bass, monkfish, red snapper or haddock

24 large raw prawns in their shells

1 raw squid

2 tbsp olive oil

1 large onion, finely chopped

1 fennel bulb, thinly sliced, feathery fronds reserved

2 large garlic cloves, crushed

4 tbsp pastis, such as Pernod

1 litre/1¾ pints fish stock

2 large sun-ripened tomatoes, peeled, deseeded and diced, or 400 g/14 oz chopped tomatoes, drained

1 tbsp tomato purée

1 bay leaf

pinch of sugar

pinch of dried chilli flakes (optional)

salt and pepper

French bread, to serve

Marseille-style Fish Stew

Use whatever fish is available, but avoid using oily fish such as mackerel and salmon, or swordfish and tuna, which are too meaty for this treatment. Scallops and mussels are suitable shellfish to use in this dish.

• Put the saffron threads in a small dry frying pan over a high heat and toast, stirring constantly for 1 minute, or until you can smell the aroma. Immediately tip out of the pan and set aside.

• Prepare the fish as necessary, removing and reserving all skin, bones and heads. Cut the flesh into large chunks. Peel and devein the prawns. Cover and refrigerate the fish and prawns until required.

• To prepare the squid, use your fingers to rub off the thin membrane that covers the body. Pull the head and insides out of the body sac, then cut off and reserve the tentacles. Pull out the thin, clear quill that is inside the body. Rinse the squid inside and out, then cut the body into 5-mm/¼-inch rings. Cover and refrigerate the squid until required.

• Heat the oil in a large, flameproof casserole or heavy-based saucepan and cook the onion and sliced fennel for 3 minutes. Add the garlic and cook for a further 5 minutes, or until the onion and fennel are softened but not browned.

• Remove the casserole from the heat. Warm the pastis in a ladle or small saucepan, ignite and pour over the onion and fennel to flambé.

• When the flames die down, return the casserole to the heat and stir in the stock, tomatoes, tomato purée, bay leaf, sugar, chilli flakes, if using, and salt and pepper to taste. Slowly bring to the boil, then reduce the heat and simmer for 15 minutes. Taste, and adjust the seasoning if necessary.

• Add the prawns and squid and simmer just until the prawns have turned pink and the squid is opaque. Using a slotted spoon, transfer the prawns and squid to warmed serving bowls.

• Add the fish to the broth and simmer just until the flesh flakes easily – not longer than 5 minutes, depending on the type of fish. Transfer the seafood and broth to the serving bowls, removing the smaller, thinner pieces first. Garnish with the reserved fennel fronds and serve with French bread.

SERVES 6

2 tbsp sunflower or corn oil

175 g/6 oz okra, trimmed and cut into
   2.5-cm/1-inch pieces

2 onions, finely chopped

4 celery sticks, very finely chopped

1 garlic clove, finely chopped

2 tbsp plain flour

½ tsp sugar

1 tsp ground cumin

700 ml/1¼ pints fish stock

1 red pepper and 1 green pepper,
   deseeded and chopped

2 large tomatoes, chopped

350 g/12 oz large raw prawns

4 tbsp chopped fresh parsley

1 tbsp chopped fresh coriander

dash of Tabasco sauce

350 g/12 oz cod or haddock fillets,
   skinned

350 g/12 oz monkfish fillet

salt and pepper

Louisiana Gumbo

To peel and devein prawns, remove the head and tail, then peel away the shell. Using a sharp knife, cut along the back of the prawn to remove the black intestinal thread that runs down the centre. Wash well.

• Heat half the oil in a large, flameproof casserole, or large saucepan with tightly fitting lid, and cook the okra over a low heat, stirring frequently, for 5 minutes, or until browned. Using a slotted spoon, remove from the casserole and set aside.

• Heat the remaining oil in the casserole and cook the onion and celery over a medium heat, stirring frequently, for 5 minutes, or until softened. Add the garlic and cook, stirring, for 1 minute. Sprinkle in the flour, sugar and cumin and add salt and pepper to taste. Cook, stirring constantly, for 2 minutes, then remove from the heat.

• Gradually stir in the stock and bring to the boil, stirring. Return the okra to the casserole and add the peppers and tomatoes. Partially cover, reduce the heat to very low and gently simmer, stirring occasionally, for 10 minutes. Meanwhile, peel and devein the prawns and reserve.

• Add the herbs and Tabasco sauce to taste. Cut the cod and monkfish into 2.5-cm/1-inch chunks, then gently stir into the stew. Stir in the prawns. Cover and gently simmer for 5 minutes, or until the fish is cooked through and the prawns have turned pink. Transfer to a large, warmed serving dish and serve.

SERVES 4

24 live mussels

24 live clams

450 g/1 lb sea bream fillets

1.5 litres/2¾ pints fish stock

225 ml/8 fl oz dry white wine

2 shallots, finely chopped

24 raw Mediterranean prawns, peeled
and deveined

700 g/1 lb 9 oz tomatoes, peeled,
deseeded and roughly chopped

3 tbsp snipped fresh chives

grated rind of 1 lemon

pinch of saffron threads

3 tbsp finely chopped fresh parsley

salt and pepper

Shellfish Stew

This dish is quite messy, so provide finger bowls filled with hot water and a slice of lemon so that your guests can wash their fingers after eating.

• Clean the mussels and clams by scrubbing or scraping the shells and pulling out any beards that are attached to the mussels. Discard any with broken shells or any that refuse to close when tapped. Cut the sea bream into bite-sized pieces.

• Pour the stock and wine into a large, heavy-based saucepan and bring to the boil. Add the mussels, clams and shallots, cover and cook over a medium heat for 4 minutes. Tip into a sieve, reserving the stock. Discard any mussels or clams that remain closed and set the remainder aside.

• Rinse the saucepan and strain the stock back into it through a muslin-lined sieve. Return to the boil and add the prawns and sea bream. Stir in the tomatoes, chives, lemon rind, saffron and parsley and season to taste with salt and pepper. Gently simmer for 10 minutes, or until the fish flakes easily when tested with the point of a knife.

• Remove the saucepan from the heat and add the mussels and clams. Cover and leave to stand for 5 minutes. Divide the stew between 4 soup bowls and serve immediately.

SERVES 4–6

200 g/7 oz dried ribbon egg pasta,
    such as tagliatelle
25 g/1 oz butter
55 g/2 oz fine fresh breadcrumbs
400 ml/14 fl oz canned condensed
    cream of mushroom soup

125 ml/4 fl oz milk
2 celery sticks, chopped
1 red pepper, deseeded and chopped
1 green pepper, deseeded and
    chopped
140 g/5 oz mature Cheddar cheese,
    coarsely grated

2 tbsp chopped fresh parsley
200 g/7 oz canned tuna in oil, drained
    and flaked
salt and pepper

Tuna & Noodle Casserole

If you like the flavour of celery, use canned condensed cream of celery soup instead of the mushroom soup and replace the celery sticks with 200 g/7 oz canned, drained sweetcorn kernels.

- Preheat the oven to 200°C/400°F/Gas Mark 6. Bring a large saucepan of salted water to the boil. Add the pasta, return to the boil and cook for 2 minutes less than specified on the packet instructions.
- Meanwhile, melt the butter in a separate small saucepan. Stir in the breadcrumbs, then remove from the heat and set aside.
- Drain the pasta well and set aside. Pour the soup into the pasta saucepan over a medium heat, then stir in the milk, celery, peppers, half the cheese and all the parsley. Add the tuna and gently stir in so that the flakes don't break up. Season to taste with salt and pepper. Heat just until small bubbles appear around the edge of the mixture – do not boil.
- Stir the pasta into the saucepan and use 2 forks to mix all the ingredients together. Spoon the mixture into an ovenproof dish that is also suitable for serving and spread it out.
- Stir the remaining cheese into the buttered breadcrumbs, then sprinkle over the top of the pasta mixture. Bake in the preheated oven for 20–25 minutes until the topping is golden. Remove from the oven, then leave to stand for 5 minutes before serving straight from the dish.

SERVES 4

225 g/8 oz live clams

225 g/8 oz live mussels

2 tbsp olive oil

1 onion, sliced

pinch of saffron threads

1 tbsp chopped fresh thyme

2 garlic cloves, finely chopped

800 g/1 lb 12 oz canned tomatoes, drained and chopped

175 ml/6 fl oz dry white wine

2 litres/3½ pints fish stock

350 g/12 oz red mullet fillets, cut into bite-sized chunks

450 g/1 lb monkfish fillet, cut into bite-sized chunks

225 g/8 oz raw squid rings

2 tbsp fresh shredded basil leaves

salt and pepper

fresh bread, to serve

Seafood in Saffron Sauce

Although saffron is very expensive, its unique aromatic flavour marries particularly well with seafood, and, in any case, you need only a tiny amount.

• Clean the mussels and clams by scrubbing or scraping the shells and pulling out any beards that are attached to the mussels. Discard any with broken shells or any that refuse to close when tapped.

• Heat the oil in a large, flameproof casserole and cook the onion with the saffron, thyme and a pinch of salt over a low heat, stirring occasionally, for 5 minutes, or until softened. Add the garlic and cook, stirring, for 2 minutes.

• Add the tomatoes, wine and stock, season to taste with salt and pepper and stir well. Bring to the boil, then reduce the heat and simmer for 15 minutes.

• Add the fish chunks and simmer for a further 3 minutes. Add the clams, mussels and squid rings and simmer for a further 5 minutes, or until the mussels and clams have opened. Discard any that remain closed. Stir in the basil and serve immediately, accompanied by plenty of fresh bread to mop up the broth.

All manner of vegetables can be used and combined to great effect in stews and casseroles, resulting in dishes that are brimming with both flavour and texture, as you will see in this chapter. Pulses – dried beans, peas and lentils – in all their wonderful variety are at the heart of many of these recipes, and the different types can be interchanged or mixed and matched according to individual preference or availability. If cooking from dried, beans and chickpeas need to be soaked in plenty of cold water for several hours or overnight. Most beans then need to be drained, covered with fresh water and boiled rapidly for 10 minutes to rid them of potentially harmful substances, before slow cooking – the exact cooking time varying according to the type and age of the beans. However, many different types of beans are conveniently available canned and ready to use, and these are also featured in some of the recipes here.

VITAL VEGETABLES

Lentils, which don't require any presoaking or cooking, take the place of meat in the Vegetable Goulash featured here, accompanied by hearty root vegetables and tender squash in a rich tomato broth. Dried haricot beans are used in the Spring Stew, but after the initial preparation, this dish is quickly put together, making the best of sweet and tender young vegetables. Canned chickpeas are complemented by aubergine, sweet potatoes and prunes in the aromatic Moroccan Hot Pot, while tofu is teamed with peppers, French beans and baby sweetcorn in the typically Thai-flavoured Fragrant Vegetable Pot. Whether for everyday eating or informal entertaining, these nutritious and delicious dishes will appeal as much to meat eaters as to vegetarians.

SERVES 4

225 g/8 oz fragrant rice

3 tbsp sunflower oil

250 g/9 oz organic firm tofu

2.5-cm/1-inch piece fresh root ginger

2 stalks lemon grass

1–2 garlic cloves

1–2 bird's eye chillies

3 shallots, cut into wedges

3 sticks celery

175 g/6 oz carrots

1 red pepper, 1 yellow pepper

600–700 ml/1–1¼ pints vegetable
    stock

2 tbsp light soy sauce

115 g/4 oz French beans

85 g/3 oz broccoli, divided into tiny
    florets

115 g/4 oz baby sweetcorn

6 spring onions

1 tbsp fresh coriander, chopped

1½ tbsp cornflour

2 tablespoons cold water

salt and pepper

long-grain rice, to serve

Fragrant Vegetable Pot

For an even greater variety
of vegetables in this dish,
add some shredded pak
choi and beansprouts with
the spring onions
and coriander.

• Bring a large saucepan of lightly salted water to the boil. Add the rice, return to the boil and cook for 12 minutes, or until tender but still firm to the bite. Drain, cover and keep warm.

• Heat 2 tablespoons of the oil in a frying pan. Cut the tofu into bite-sized cubes, add to the pan and cook over a low heat, stirring frequently, for 8–10 minutes, until golden on all sides. Remove and set aside.

• Peel and grate the ginger. Remove the outer leaves of the lemon grass and discard. Finely chop the stalks, crush the garlic, and deseed and chop the chillies. Heat the remaining oil in a large, heavy-based saucepan and cook the ginger, lemon grass, garlic and chillies, stirring frequently, for 3 minutes. Cut the celery into 5-mm/¼-inch slices, and add to the pan with shallots. Cook, stirring, for 2 minutes.

• Cut the carrots into batons, then deseed the peppers and cut them into small chunks. Add the carrots, peppers, 450 ml/16 fl oz of the stock and soy sauce to the saucepan, then bring to the boil. Reduce the heat, cover and simmer for 10 minutes.

• Halve the French beans, and add them to the pan with the broccoli, sweetcorn and the remaining stock and simmer for a further 5 minutes. Add the tofu, spring onions and coriander and season to taste with pepper.

• Blend the cornflour with the water, stir into the saucepan and cook, stirring gently to avoid breaking up the vegetables, for 2 minutes, or until the liquid is thickened. Serve with long-grain rice.

SERVES 4

425 g/15 oz canned chickpeas

4 tomatoes, peeled and deseeded

700 ml/1¼ pints vegetable stock

1 onion, sliced

2 carrots, diagonally sliced

1 tbsp chopped fresh coriander

175 g/6 oz courgettes, sliced

1 small turnip, cubed

½ tsp ground turmeric

¼ tsp ground ginger

¼ tsp ground cinnamon

225 g/8 oz couscous

salt

fresh sprigs of coriander, to garnish

Moroccan Vegetable Stew

To peel tomatoes, cut a cross through the skin at the base of each tomato, put in a heatproof bowl and pour over boiling water. Leave for a couple of minutes, then drain and plunge into cold water. The skins will peel off easily.

• Drain the chickpeas, rinse under cold running water, drain again and set aside.

• Roughly chop the tomatoes and reserve half. Put the remainder in a blender or food processor and process until smooth. Transfer to a large saucepan and add 400 ml/¾ pint of the stock. Bring to the boil, then reduce the heat and add the onion, carrots, chopped coriander, and salt to taste. Simmer, stirring occasionally, for 10 minutes.

• Stir in the courgettes, turnip, spices and the reserved tomatoes. Partially cover and simmer for a further 30 minutes. Stir in the chickpeas and simmer for a further 5 minutes.

• Meanwhile, bring the remaining stock to the boil in a large, heavy-based saucepan with a tight-fitting lid. Add a pinch of salt, then sprinkle in the couscous, stirring constantly. Remove the saucepan from the heat, cover and leave to stand for 5 minutes. Fluff the couscous up with a fork and transfer to 4 serving plates.

• Top with the vegetables and their stock, garnish with coriander sprigs and serve immediately.

SERVES 4

1 large fennel bulb

2 tbsp olive oil

1 red onion, cut into small wedges

2–4 garlic cloves, sliced

1 fresh green chilli, deseeded and
chopped

1 small aubergine, about 225 g/8 oz,
cut into chunks

2 tbsp tomato purée

450–600 ml/16 fl oz–1 pint vegetable
stock

450 g/1 lb ripe tomatoes

1 tbsp balsamic vinegar

few fresh sprigs of oregano

400 g/14 oz canned borlotti beans

400 g/14 oz canned flageolet beans

1 yellow pepper, deseeded and cut
into small strips

1 courgette, sliced into half moons

55 g/2 oz stoned black olives

25 g/1 oz Parmesan cheese, freshly
shaved

salt and pepper

polenta wedges or crusty bread,
to serve

Tuscan Bean Stew

Fennel, also known as
Florence fennel, has an
aniseed flavour that is
excellent when combined
with tomatoes, garlic and
chilli. If not available, try
using some crushed fennel
seeds and fry them with
the onion and garlic.

• Trim the fennel and reserve any feathery fronds, then cut the bulb into small strips. Heat the oil in a large, heavy-based saucepan with a tight-fitting lid, and cook the onion, garlic, chilli and fennel strips, stirring frequently, for 5–8 minutes, or until softened.

• Add the aubergine and cook, stirring frequently, for 5 minutes. Blend the tomato purée with a little of the stock in a jug and pour over the fennel mixture, then add the remaining stock, and the tomatoes, vinegar and oregano. Bring to the boil, then reduce the heat, cover and simmer for 15 minutes, or until the tomatoes have begun to collapse.

• Drain and rinse the beans, then drain again. Add them to the pan with the yellow pepper, courgette and olives. Simmer for a further 15 minutes, or until all the vegetables are tender. Taste and adjust the seasoning. Scatter with the Parmesan cheese shavings and serve garnished with the reserved fennel fronds, accompanied by polenta wedges or crusty bread.

SERVES 4

4 garlic cloves

1 small acorn squash

1 red onion, sliced

2 leeks, sliced

1 aubergine, sliced

1 small celeriac, diced

2 turnips, sliced

2 plum tomatoes, chopped

1 carrot, sliced

1 courgette, sliced

2 red peppers

1 fennel bulb, sliced

175 g/6 oz chard

2 bay leaves

½ tsp fennel seeds

½ tsp chilli powder

pinch each of dried thyme, dried oregano and sugar

125 ml/4 fl oz extra virgin olive oil

225 ml/8 fl oz vegetable stock

25 g/1 oz fresh basil leaves, torn

4 tbsp chopped fresh parsley

salt and pepper

2 tbsp freshly grated Parmesan cheese, to serve

Italian Vegetable Stew

Unless you are using pulses, nuts or grains, it is a good idea to complement vegetable dishes with a little cheese to provide some protein.

• Finely chop the garlic and dice the squash. Put them in a large, heavy-based saucepan with a tight-fitting lid. Add the onion, leeks, aubergine, celeriac, turnips, tomatoes, carrot, courgette, red peppers, fennel, chard, bay leaves, fennel seeds, chilli powder, thyme, oregano, sugar, oil, stock and half the basil. Mix together well, then bring to the boil.

• Reduce the heat, cover and simmer for 30 minutes, or until all the vegetables are tender.

• Sprinkle in the remaining basil and the parsley and season to taste with salt and pepper. Serve immediately, sprinkled with the cheese.

SERVES 4–6

115 g/4 oz dried kidney beans

115 g/4 oz dried chickpeas

115 g/4 oz dried haricot beans

2 tbsp olive oil

1 onion, chopped

2–4 garlic cloves, chopped

2 fresh red chillies, deseeded and
sliced

1 tbsp tomato purée

700–850 ml/1¼–1½ pints vegetable
stock

1 red pepper, deseeded and chopped

4 tomatoes, roughly chopped

175 g/6 oz frozen or shelled fresh
broad beans, thawed if frozen

1 tbsp chopped fresh coriander

pepper

soured cream, to serve

fresh sprigs of coriander and a pinch
of paprika, to garnish

Chilli Bean Stew

If time is short, take a shortcut and instead of the dried beans use double the quantity of canned beans. Disregard the first paragraph and begin at paragraph 2, adding the canned, drained beans in place of the drained, soaked beans. Once the stock is reduced to a simmer, skip the 50 minutes' simmering and move straight on to paragraph 3.

• Pick over the beans and chickpeas, rinse thoroughly, drain and put in separate bowls. Cover with plenty of cold water and leave to soak overnight. The next day, drain, put in separate saucepans and cover with cold water. Bring to the boil and boil rapidly for 10 minutes, then drain and set aside.

• Heat the oil in a large, heavy-based saucepan with a tight-fitting lid, and cook the onion, garlic and chillies, stirring frequently, for 5 minutes, or until softened. Add the drained soaked beans. Blend the tomato purée with a little of the stock in a jug and pour over the bean mixture, then add the remaining stock. Bring to the boil, then reduce the heat, cover and simmer, stirring occasionally, for 50 minutes, or until the beans are almost tender.

• Add the red pepper, tomatoes, broad beans, and pepper to taste and simmer for a further 15–20 minutes, or until the beans are thoroughly cooked. Stir in the chopped coriander. Serve the stew topped with spoonfuls of soured cream and garnished with sprigs of coriander and a pinch of paprika.

SERVES 4

350 g/12 oz dried pinto beans, covered with cold water and soaked overnight

2 tbsp olive oil

2 onions, sliced

2 garlic cloves, finely chopped

1 red pepper, deseeded and sliced

1 yellow pepper, deseeded and sliced

400 g/14 oz canned chopped tomatoes

2 tbsp tomato purée

1 tbsp torn fresh basil leaves

2 tsp chopped fresh thyme

2 tsp chopped fresh rosemary

1 bay leaf

55 g/2 oz black olives, stoned and halved

salt and pepper

2 tbsp chopped fresh parsley, to garnish

Provençal Bean Stew

Always follow the packet instructions for soaking and cooking the particular type of bean you are using.

If you use borlotti beans instead of the pinto beans, you will need to boil them vigorously for 10 minutes before simmering.

• Drain the beans and put in a large, heavy-based saucepan with a tight-fitting lid, add enough cold water to cover and bring to the boil. Reduce the heat, cover and simmer for 1¼–1½ hours, or until almost tender. Drain, reserving 300 ml/10 fl oz of the cooking liquid.

• Heat the oil in another large, heavy-based saucepan with a tight-fitting lid, and cook the onions, stirring frequently, for 5 minutes, or until softened. Add the garlic and peppers and cook, stirring frequently, for 10 minutes.

• Add the tomatoes and their can juices, the reserved cooking liquid, tomato purée, herbs and beans and season to taste with salt and pepper. Cover and simmer for 40 minutes. Add the olives and simmer for a further 5 minutes. Transfer to a warmed serving dish, sprinkle with the parsley and serve immediately.

SERVES 4

225 g/8 oz dried haricot beans

2 tbsp olive oil

4–8 baby onions, halved

2 celery sticks, cut into 5-mm/¼-inch slices

225 g/8 oz baby carrots, scrubbed and halved if large

300 g/10½ oz new potatoes, scrubbed and halved, or quartered if large

850 ml–1.2 litres/1½–2 pints vegetable stock

1 fresh bouquet garni

1½–2 tbsp light soy sauce

85 g/3 oz baby sweetcorn

115 g/4 oz frozen or shelled fresh broad beans, thawed if frozen

½–1 Savoy or spring (Primo) cabbage, about 225 g/8 oz

1½ tbsp cornflour

2 tbsp cold water

salt and pepper

55–85 g/2–3 oz Parmesan or mature Cheddar cheese, grated, to serve

Spring Stew

Although not as widely available as some other varieties of cabbage, savoy cabbage's delicate flavour makes it ideal for cooking.

• Pick over the haricot beans, rinse thoroughly, drain and put in a large bowl. Cover with plenty of cold water and leave to soak overnight. The next day, drain, put in a saucepan and cover with cold water. Bring to the boil and boil rapidly for 10 minutes, then drain and set aside.

• Heat the oil in a large, heavy-based saucepan with a tight-fitting lid, and cook the vegetables, stirring frequently, for 5 minutes, or until softened. Add the stock, drained beans, bouquet garni and soy sauce, then bring to the boil. Reduce the heat, cover and simmer for 12 minutes.

• Add the baby sweetcorn and broad beans and season to taste with salt and pepper. Simmer for a further 3 minutes.

• Meanwhile, discard the outer leaves and hard central core from the cabbage and shred the leaves. Add to the saucepan and simmer for a further 3–5 minutes, or until all the vegetables are tender.

• Blend the cornflour with the water, stir into the saucepan and cook, stirring, for 4–6 minutes, or until the liquid has thickened. Serve the cheese separately, for stirring into the stew.

SERVES 4

10 cloves

1 onion, peeled but kept whole

225 g/8 oz Puy or green lentils

1 bay leaf

1.5 litres/2¾ pints vegetable stock

2 leeks, sliced

2 potatoes, diced

2 carrots, chopped

3 courgettes, sliced

1 celery stick, chopped

1 red pepper, deseeded and chopped

1 tbsp lemon juice

salt and pepper

Vegetable & Lentil Casserole

Ordinary green lentils are fine to use in this dish, but the Puy lentil, originating from the south of France, is regarded as the king of lentils. Puy lentils have a superior refined flavour and always retain their shape and texture.

• Preheat the oven to 180°C/350°F/Gas Mark 4. Press the cloves into the onion. Put the lentils into a large casserole, add the onion and bay leaf and pour in the stock. Cover and cook in the preheated oven for 1 hour.
• Remove the onion and discard the cloves. Slice the onion and return it to the casserole with the vegetables. Stir thoroughly and season to taste with salt and pepper. Cover and return to the oven for 1 hour.
• Discard the bay leaf. Stir in the lemon juice and serve straight from the casserole.

SERVES 4

15 g/½ oz sun-dried tomatoes,
  chopped
225 g/8 oz Puy lentils
600 ml/1 pint cold water
2 tbsp olive oil
½–1 tsp crushed dried chillies
2–3 garlic cloves, chopped

1 large onion, cut into small wedges
1 small celeriac, cut into small chunks
225 g/8 oz carrots, sliced
225 g/8 oz new potatoes, scrubbed
  and cut into chunks
1 small acorn squash, deseeded,
  peeled and cut into small chunks,
  about 225 g/8 oz prepared weight

2 tbsp tomato purée
300 ml/10 fl oz vegetable stock
1–2 tsp hot paprika
few fresh sprigs of thyme
450 g/1 lb ripe tomatoes
soured cream and crusty bread,
  to serve

Vegetable Goulash

If the squash is not available, you could use the same quantity of sweet potatoes or parsnips, cut into small chunks.

• Put the sun-dried tomatoes in a small heatproof bowl, cover with almost boiling water and leave to soak for 15–20 minutes. Drain, reserving the soaking liquid. Meanwhile, rinse and drain the lentils, and put them in a saucepan with the cold water and bring to the boil. Reduce the heat, cover and simmer for 15 minutes. Drain and set aside.

• Heat the oil in a large, heavy-based saucepan with a tight-fitting lid, and cook the chillies, garlic and vegetables, stirring frequently, for 5–8 minutes until softened. Blend the tomato purée with a little of the stock in a jug and pour over the vegetable mixture, then add the remaining stock, lentils, the sun-dried tomatoes and their soaking liquid, and the paprika and thyme.

• Bring to the boil, then reduce the heat, cover and simmer for 15 minutes. Add the fresh tomatoes and simmer for a further 15 minutes, or until the vegetables and lentils are tender. Serve topped with spoonfuls of soured cream, accompanied by crusty bread.

SERVES 4

1 Spanish onion

2 tbsp olive oil

2–4 garlic cloves, crushed

1 fresh red chilli, deseeded and sliced

1 aubergine, about 225 g/8 oz,
    cut into small chunks

small piece fresh root ginger, peeled
    and grated

1 tsp ground cumin

1 tsp ground coriander

pinch of saffron threads or
    ½ tsp turmeric

1–2 cinnamon sticks

½–1 butternut squash, about
    450 g/1 lb, peeled, deseeded and
    cut into small chunks

225 g/8 oz sweet potatoes, cut into
    small chunks

85 g/3 oz ready-to-eat prunes

450–600 ml/16 fl oz–1 pint vegetable
    stock

4 tomatoes, chopped

400 g/14 oz canned chickpeas,
    drained and rinsed

1 tbsp chopped fresh coriander,
    to garnish

Moroccan Hot Pot

If you like, sprinkle over some chopped ready-to-eat dried apricots or the seeds from a pomegranate before serving. Freshly prepared couscous or bulgar wheat would be ideal to serve with this stew.

• Finely chop the onion. Heat the oil in a large, heavy-based saucepan with a tight-fitting lid, and cook the onion, garlic, chilli and aubergine, stirring frequently, for 5–8 minutes until softened.

• Add the ginger, cumin, ground coriander and saffron and cook, stirring constantly, for 2 minutes. Bruise the cinnamon stick.

• Add the cinnamon, squash, sweet potatoes, prunes, stock and tomatoes to the saucepan and bring to the boil. Reduce the heat, cover and simmer, stirring occasionally, for 20 minutes.

• Add the chickpeas to the saucepan and cook for a further 10 minutes. Discard the cinnamon and serve garnished with the fresh coriander.

There are few things in life as traditional and satisfying as enjoying a home-cooked roast dinner, and the following pages contain over 30 of the finest dishes for you to try. You will discover a range of delightful recipes, from the old favourite roast beef and festive feasts such as roast duck and turkey, to culinary treats such as fillets of tuna cooked with orange, and mouth-watering squab chickens roasted with herbs and wine.

Vegetarians are catered for with delicious roasted vegetables including crispy roast asparagus and the perfect roast potatoes, which also make ideal side dishes to accompany the main feast. Gathering people together for a Sunday lunch is one of the nicest ways to spend time with friends and family, and you are sure to find something to please everyone in the collection of classic and contemporary dishes that follow.

and a smaller one in which vegetables and fish fillets can fit snugly. If the tin is too large for its contents, fat will spit messily all over the inside of the oven. If it's too small, cooking may be uneven and fat can spill over the sides, risking a dangerous fire. If the tins are heavyweight, they ensure even cooking and last a lifetime.

A good, flexible carving knife with a blade 30-35–cm/12-14–inches long is also essential and a knife sharpener will keep it in good condition. Always allow roast meat to stand, tented with foil to keep it warm, for 10–20 minutes after removing it from the oven. This evens out the residual heat and stabilizes the texture, making it easier to carve into neat slices. A carving fork is not essential, but is a worthwhile safety feature.

INTRODUCTION TO
ROASTING

Roasting is the technique of cooking in radiant heat and it can be used for a wide variety of ingredients, including meat, poultry, game, fish and vegetables. All the recipes in the following chapters have been tested in conventional ovens, so you won't have to worry about buying expensive gadgets, such as rotisseries for spit roasting, and they work just as successfully whatever fuel you are using in your kitchen.

It's unlikely you will need to rush out and buy any other extra equipment either. It's worth having a couple of good-quality, heavy roasting tins – a larger one for a turkey or a rib of beef

Meat is the most popular ingredient for roasting and the traditional favourite for family meals. While the classic Sunday roast fell out of favour for a time, it is enjoying renewed popularity, especially now that leaner cuts are widely available. However, do bear in mind that some fat is necessary to keep the meat moist during cooking and to intensify the flavour.

Lamb is the perfect choice for spring, although it is available throughout the year. Leg is ideal if you are feeding a number of guests and rack of lamb looks attractive as well as being easy to carve. Shoulder is often said to have the sweetest meat, but it is more awkward to carve. However, you can buy it boned and rolled. Lamb is usually served while still pink in the middle.

It is not a coincidence that the French nicknamed the British 'les rosbifs' as beef has been a favourite roast for centuries. For oven

FROM THE CARVERY

roasting, larger joints are best, particularly rib. Fillet may be roasted for special occasions, but it must be well larded and basted frequently during cooking. Slightly tougher cuts, such as brisket and topside, are suitable for the slower method of pot roasting.

There are many different cuts of pork in a wide range of sizes that are suitable for roasting. Perhaps the most popular is boned and rolled loin, as it is very tender and easy to carve, while leg is an economical buy if you are feeding a large number of people. Unlike lamb and beef, pork must always be well cooked. Check by piercing it with a skewer to see if the juices run clear. Alternatively, use a meat thermometer. It is done when this registers 80°C/176°F.

SERVES 8

1 prime rib of beef joint, weighing
   2.7 kg/6 lb

2 tsp dry English mustard

3 tbsp plain flour

300 ml/10 fl oz red wine

300 ml/10 fl oz beef stock

2 tsp Worcestershire sauce (optional)

salt and pepper

Yorkshire puddings, to serve

Roast Beef

Roast beef is a difficult roast to get right because, unlike most other meats, how well cooked the meat should be is very much a case of personal preference. The best roast beef is a rib cooked on the bone, but this must be a good size.

• Preheat the oven to 230°C/450°F/Gas Mark 8.

• Season the meat to taste with salt and pepper. Rub in the mustard and 1 tablespoon of the flour. Place the meat in a roasting tin large enough to hold it comfortably and roast in the oven for 15 minutes. Reduce the temperature to 190°C/375°F/Gas Mark 5 and cook for 15 minutes per 450 g/1 lb, plus 15 minutes (1¾ hours for this joint) for rare beef or 20 minutes per 450 g/1 lb, plus 20 minutes (2 hours 20 minutes) for medium beef. Baste the meat from time to time to keep it moist, and if the tin becomes too dry, add a little stock or red wine.

• Remove the meat from the oven and place on a warmed serving plate, cover with foil and leave in a warm place for 10–15 minutes.

• To make the gravy, pour off most of the fat from the tin (reserve it for cooking the Yorkshire pudding), leaving behind the meat juices and the sediment. Place the tin on the hob over a medium heat and scrape all the sediment from the base of the tin. Sprinkle in the remaining flour and quickly mix it into the juices with a small whisk. When you have a smooth paste, gradually add the wine and most of the stock, whisking constantly. Bring to the boil, then reduce the heat to a gentle simmer and cook for 2–3 minutes. Season to taste with salt and pepper and add the remaining stock, if needed, and a little Worcestershire sauce, if you like.

• When ready to serve, carve the meat into slices and serve on warmed plates. Pour the gravy into a warmed jug and take direct to the table. Serve with Yorkshire puddings.

SERVES 6

2½ tbsp plain flour

1 tsp salt

¼ tsp pepper

1 rolled brisket joint, weighing
    1.6 kg/3 lb 8 oz

2 tbsp vegetable oil

2 tbsp butter

1 onion, finely chopped

2 celery sticks, diced

2 carrots, peeled and diced

1 tsp dill seed

1 tsp dried thyme or oregano

350 ml/12 fl oz red wine

150–225 ml/5–8 fl oz beef stock

4–5 potatoes, cut into large chunks
    and boiled until just tender

2 tbsp chopped fresh dill, to serve

Beef Pot Roast with Potatoes & Dill

When using a flour and butter paste, also known as beurre manié, to thicken a sauce or gravy, whisk it into the sauce in small pieces, making sure each piece has been blended in before adding the next.

• Preheat the oven to 140°C/275°F/Gas Mark 1.

• Mix 2 tablespoons of the flour with the salt and pepper in a shallow dish. Dip the meat to coat. Heat the oil in a flameproof casserole and brown the meat all over. Transfer to a plate.

• Add half the butter to the casserole and cook the onion, celery, carrots, dill seed and thyme for 5 minutes. Return the meat and juices to the casserole.

• Pour in the wine and enough stock to reach one third of the way up the meat. Bring to the boil, cover and cook in the oven for 3 hours, turning the meat every 30 minutes. After it has been cooking for 2 hours, add the potatoes and more stock if necessary.

• When ready, transfer the meat and vegetables to a warmed serving dish. Strain the cooking liquid into a saucepan.

• Mix the remaining butter and flour to a paste. Bring the cooking liquid to the boil. Whisk in small pieces of the flour and butter paste, whisking constantly until the sauce is smooth. Pour the sauce over the meat and vegetables. Sprinkle with the fresh dill to serve.

SERVES 2

1 trimmed rack of lamb, weighing
  250–300 g/9–10½ oz
1 garlic clove, crushed
150 ml/5 fl oz red wine
1 fresh rosemary sprig, crushed to
  release the flavour
1 tbsp olive oil
150 ml/5 fl oz lamb stock

2 tbsp redcurrant jelly
salt and pepper

MINT SAUCE
bunch fresh mint leaves
2 tsp caster sugar
2 tbsp water
2 tbsp white wine vinegar

Rack Of Lamb

Lamb is best in spring, from Easter onwards, when it is at its sweetest and most succulent. Rosemary and garlic are traditional flavourings and a gravy made with red wine and redcurrant jelly is divine. Fresh mint for sauce is also at its best around this time. Rack of lamb is an impressive dish for entertaining, too. Just double or treble the ingredients, depending on the number of guests.

• Place the rack of lamb in a non-metallic bowl and rub all over with the garlic. Pour over the wine and place the rosemary sprig on top. Cover and leave to marinate in the refrigerator for 3 hours or overnight if possible.

• Preheat the oven to 220°C/425°F/Gas Mark 7. Remove the lamb from the marinade, reserving the marinade. Pat the meat dry with kitchen paper and season well with salt and pepper. Place it in a small roasting tin, drizzle with the oil and roast for 15–20 minutes, depending on whether you like your meat pink or medium. Remove the lamb from the oven and leave to rest, covered with foil, in a warm place for 5 minutes.

• Meanwhile, pour the reserved marinade into a small saucepan, bring to the boil over a medium heat and bubble gently for 2–3 minutes. Add the stock and redcurrant jelly and simmer, stirring, until the mixture is syrupy.

• To make the mint sauce, chop the fresh mint leaves and mix together with the sugar in a small bowl. Add the boiling water and stir to dissolve the sugar. Add the white wine vinegar and leave to stand for 30 minutes before serving with the lamb.

• Carve the lamb into cutlets and serve on warmed plates with the sauce spooned over the top. Serve the Mint Sauce separately.

SERVES 4

1 leg of lamb, weighing
   1.6 kg/3 lb 8 oz
3–4 fresh rosemary sprigs
115 g/4 oz streaky bacon rashers
4 tbsp olive oil
2–3 garlic cloves, crushed
2 onions, sliced

2 carrots, sliced
2 celery sticks, sliced
300 ml/10 fl oz dry white wine
1 tbsp tomato purée
300 ml/10 fl oz lamb or chicken stock
3 medium tomatoes, peeled,
   quartered and deseeded
1 tbsp chopped fresh parsley

1 tbsp chopped fresh oregano
   or marjoram
salt and pepper
fresh rosemary sprigs, to garnish

Leg of Lamb Pot Roast

This dish from the Abruzzi region of Italy uses a slow cooking method. The meat absorbs the flavourings and becomes very tender.

- Wipe the lamb all over with kitchen paper, trim off any excess fat and season to taste with salt and pepper, rubbing well in. Lay the sprigs of rosemary over the lamb, evenly cover and securely tie in place with kitchen string.
- Heat the oil in a frying pan and fry the lamb over a medium heat for 10 minutes, turning several times. Remove from the pan.
- Preheat the oven to 160°C/325°F/Gas Mark 3. Transfer the oil from the frying pan to a large flameproof casserole and cook the garlic and onions for 3–4 minutes until the onions are beginning to soften. Add the carrots and celery and cook for a further few minutes.
- Lay the lamb on top of the vegetables and press down to partly submerge. Pour the wine over the lamb, add the tomato purée and simmer for 3–4 minutes. Add the stock, tomatoes and herbs and season to taste with salt and pepper. Return to the boil for a further 3–4 minutes.
- Lightly cover the casserole and cook in the oven for 2–2½ hours until very tender.
- Remove the lamb from the casserole and, if you like, remove the bacon and herbs together with the string. Keep the lamb warm. Strain the juices, skimming off any excess fat, and serve in a jug. The vegetables may be put around the joint or in a dish. Garnish with sprigs of rosemary.

SERVES 6

1 leg of lamb, weighing 1.8 kg/4 lb

2 garlic cloves, thinly sliced

2 tbsp fresh or dried rosemary leaves

8 tbsp olive oil

900 g/2 lb potatoes, cut into
2.5-cm/1-inch cubes

6 fresh sage leaves, chopped

150 ml/5 fl oz Marsala

salt and pepper

Roast Lamb with Rosemary & Marsala

Serving tender spring lamb on Easter Sunday to celebrate the end of the Lenten fast is traditional throughout the Mediterranean, not least in Italy where this dish originates.

• Preheat the oven to 220°C/425°F/Gas Mark 7.

• Use a small, sharp knife to make incisions all over the lamb, opening them out slightly to make little pockets. Insert the garlic slices and about half the rosemary leaves in the pockets.

• Place the lamb in a roasting tin and spoon over half the oil. Roast in the oven for 15 minutes.

• Reduce the oven temperature to 180°C/350°F/Gas Mark 4. Remove the lamb from the oven and season to taste with salt and pepper. Turn the lamb over, return it to the oven and roast for a further hour.

• Meanwhile, spread out the cubed potatoes in a second roasting tin, pour the remaining oil over them and toss to coat. Sprinkle with the remaining rosemary and the sage. Place the potatoes in the oven with the lamb and roast for 40 minutes.

• Remove the lamb from the oven, turn it over and pour over the Marsala. Return it to the oven with the potatoes and cook for a further 15 minutes. Transfer the lamb to a carving board and cover with foil. Place the roasting tin over a high heat and bring the juices to the boil. Continue to boil until thickened and syrupy. Strain into a warmed sauce boat or jug.

• Carve the lamb into slices and serve with the potatoes and sauce.

SERVES 6

1 boneless gammon joint, weighing
   1.3 kg/3 lb, pre-soaked if necessary
2 tbsp Dijon mustard
85 g/3 oz demerara sugar
½ tsp ground cinnamon
½ tsp ground ginger
18 whole cloves

CUMBERLAND SAUCE

2 Seville oranges, halved
4 tbsp redcurrant jelly
4 tbsp port
1 tsp mustard
salt and pepper

Roast Gammon

Roast gammon or ham has long been a favourite choice for Sunday lunch and for Boxing Day dinner. Both gammon and ham are salted, either by salt curing or soaking in brine, and some varieties, such as York ham, may be smoked. Some joints may need to be soaked in cold water for 2 hours or overnight to reduce the saltiness (check with your butcher, or on the packaging, to see if it has been pre-soaked). The sweet glaze of hams, or the serving of a sweet accompaniment such as Cumberland sauce, is to counteract the salt.

• Place the joint in a large saucepan, cover with cold water and gradually bring to the boil over a low heat. Cover and simmer very gently for 1 hour. Preheat the oven to 200°C/400°F/Gas Mark 6.

• Remove the gammon from the saucepan and drain. Remove the rind from the gammon and discard. Score the fat into a diamond-shaped pattern with a sharp knife.

• Spread the mustard over the fat. Mix the sugar and ground spices together on a plate and roll the gammon in it, pressing down to coat evenly.

• Stud the diamond shapes with cloves and place the joint in a roasting tin. Roast in the oven for 20 minutes until the glaze is a rich golden colour.

• To serve hot, cover with foil and leave to stand for 20 minutes before carving. If the gammon is to be served cold, it can be cooked a day ahead. Serve with Cumberland Sauce.

• To make the sauce, use a citrus zester to remove the zest of the oranges. Place the redcurrant jelly, port and mustard in a small saucepan and gently heat until the jelly has melted. Squeeze the juice from the oranges into the saucepan. Add the orange zest and season to taste with salt and pepper. Serve cold with gammon. The sauce can be kept in a screw-top jar in the refrigerator for up to 2 weeks.

SERVES 6

1 piece of loin of pork, weighing
   1.6 kg/3 lb 8 oz, boned and rolled
4 garlic cloves, thinly sliced
   lengthways
1½ tsp finely chopped fennel fronds
   or ½ tsp dried fennel

4 cloves
300 ml/10 fl oz dry white wine
300 ml/10 fl oz water
salt and pepper

Slow-Roasted Pork

Ready-prepared boned
and rolled loin of
pork is available from
supermarkets and butchers,
or you can ask your butcher
to prepare one especially
for you.

- Preheat the oven to 150°C/300°F/Gas Mark 2.
- Use a small, sharp knife to make incisions all over the pork, opening them out slightly to make little pockets. Place the garlic slices in a small sieve and rinse under cold running water to moisten. Spread out the fennel on a saucer and roll the garlic slices in it to coat. Slide the garlic slices and the cloves into the pockets in the pork. Season the meat all over to taste with salt and pepper.
- Place the pork in a large ovenproof dish or roasting tin. Pour in the wine and water. Cook in the oven, basting the meat occasionally, for 2½–2¾ hours, until the pork is tender but still quite moist.
- If you are serving the pork hot, transfer it to a carving board, cover with foil and leave to rest before cutting it into slices. If you are serving it cold, leave it to cool completely in the cooking juices before removing and slicing.

SERVES 4

1 piece of loin of pork, weighing
    1 kg/2 lb 4 oz, boned and the rind
    removed and reserved

2 tbsp mustard

1 tbsp flour

300 ml/10 fl oz cider, apple juice
    or chicken stock

salt and pepper

Apple Sauce, to serve

Roast Pork with Crackling

Roast pork can be delicious or disappointing. It is all to do with the quality of the pork and whether the fat will 'crackle' properly. The crackling is all important. It is the favourite part of the joint, and unless it is crisp and crunchy, the whole meal will be a disappointment. The best joints of pork for roasting are the leg and the loin. Choose the leg if you are catering for large numbers, although the loin, which can be bought in smaller sizes, is the best for crackling.

• Preheat the oven to 200°C/400°F/Gas Mark 6.

• Thoroughly score the pork with a sharp knife and sprinkle with salt. Place it on a wire rack on a baking tray and roast in the oven for 30–40 minutes until the crackling is golden brown and crisp. This can be cooked in advance, leaving room in the oven for roast potatoes.

• Season the pork well with salt and pepper and spread the fat with the mustard. Place in a roasting tin and roast in the centre of the oven for 20 minutes. Reduce the oven temperature to 190°C/375°F/Gas Mark 5 and cook for a further 50–60 minutes until the meat is a good colour and the juices run clear when it is pierced with a skewer.

• Remove the meat from the oven and place on a warmed serving plate, cover with foil and leave in a warm place.

• To make the gravy, pour off most of the fat from the roasting tin, leaving the meat juices and the sediment. Place the tin over a low heat. Sprinkle in the flour, whisking well. Cook the paste for a couple of minutes, then add the cider a little at a time until you have a smooth gravy. Boil for 2–3 minutes until it is the required consistency. Season well with salt and pepper and pour into a warmed serving jug.

• Carve the pork into slices and serve on warmed plates with pieces of the crackling and the gravy. Accompany with Apple Sauce.

• To make the apple sauce, peel, core and slice 450 g/1 lb Bramley apples into a medium saucepan. Add 3 tablespoons water and 15 g/½ oz caster sugar and cook over a low heat for 10 minutes, stirring occasionally. A little ground cinnamon can be added, as can 15 g/½ oz butter, if you like. Beat well until the sauce is thick and smooth – use a hand mixer for a really smooth finish.

SERVES 4–6

1 piece of pork shoulder, weighing
    900 g/2 lb, boned and trimmed,
    but left in 1 piece
225 ml/8 fl oz dry white wine
6 garlic cloves, crushed
2 dried ancho or pasilla chillies
about 4 tbsp olive oil
2 large onions, chopped

4 red or green peppers, or a mixture,
    grilled, peeled, deseeded and
    sliced
½ tsp hot paprika
800 g/1 lb 12 oz canned chopped
    tomatoes
2 fresh thyme sprigs
2 fresh parsley sprigs
salt and pepper

Pork with Sweet Peppers

Cooking 'al chilindrón' is popular throughout Spain, but it was originally from the northern regions of Navarre and Aragon, where the rugged conditions demanded hearty, full-flavoured dishes. The dried chillies in this recipe provide a close-to-authentic fiery flavour, so for a milder dish, use dried ñora chillies. You need to marinate the pork for at least 8 hours, preferably overnight.

• Place the pork in a non-metallic bowl. Pour over the wine and add 4 of the garlic cloves. Cover with clingfilm and leave to marinate in the refrigerator for at least 8 hours.

• Put the chillies in a heatproof bowl and pour over enough boiling water to cover. Leave for 20 minutes to soften, then deseed and chop. Set them aside.

• Preheat the oven to 160°C/325°F/Gas Mark 3.

• Heat 4 tablespoons of oil in a large, heavy-based flameproof casserole over a medium–high heat. Add the onions and fry for 3 minutes, then add the remaining garlic, chopped chillies, pepper slices and paprika and fry for a further 2 minutes until the onions are soft, but not brown. Use a slotted spoon to transfer the mixture to a plate, leaving as much oil as possible in the base of the casserole.

• Drain the pork, reserving the marinade, and pat dry. Add the pork to the casserole, and fry until brown on both sides.

• Return the onion mixture to the casserole with the pork and stir in the reserved marinade, tomatoes and their can juices, the herbs and salt and pepper to taste. Bring to the boil, scraping any glazed bits from the base of the pan. Cover, transfer the casserole to the oven and cook for 1 hour, or until the pork is tender. If the juices are too thin, remove the pork from the casserole and keep warm. Put the casserole over a high heat and let the juices bubble until reduced.

• Taste and adjust the seasoning. Cut the pork into serving pieces and serve with the peppers and sauce from the casserole.

It is hard to believe that a couple of generations ago, roast chicken was a rare and expensive treat reserved for special occasions.

Modern farming methods have made it much less costly and more routine, often at the expense of both flavour and texture.

However, good-quality, free-range chicken still has that special magic and remains a family favourite. Poussins, also known as

spring chicken, are popular and fun to serve, each bird providing a single portion.

Turkey has been the first choice for feeding large gatherings for a long time and that Dickensian favourite, goose, while rather

expensive, has made a great comeback in recent years.

POULTRY & GAME

All kinds of game are now much more widely available, as venison and feathered game are increasingly farmed. Fresh game

remains a seasonal treat, but it is often available frozen all year round. Like poultry, frozen game should be thoroughly thawed

before cooking. These days, most game is sold oven-ready, so you don't have to endure the time-consuming, tricky and messy tasks

of plucking and drawing it yourself. Roast pheasant, guinea fowl or a saddle of venison still retain an air of being extra special, so

they are ideal for dinner parties. Quail are also an excellent choice as they cook very quickly, taste wonderful and are much meatier

than their size would suggest.

SERVES 6

1 free-range chicken, weighing
    2.25 kg/5 lb

55 g/2 oz butter

2 tbsp chopped fresh lemon thyme

1 lemon, quartered

125 ml/4 fl oz white wine

salt and pepper

6 fresh thyme sprigs, to garnish

Roast Chicken

Simply roasted, with lots of thyme and lemon, chicken produces a succulent gastronomic feast for many occasions. Try to buy a good fresh chicken as frozen birds do not have as much flavour. You can stuff your chicken with a traditional stuffing, such as sage and onion, or fruit like apricots and prunes, but often the best way is to keep it simple.

• Preheat the oven to 220°C/425°F/Gas Mark 7. Make sure the chicken is clean, wiping it inside and out using kitchen paper, and place in a roasting tin.

• Place the butter in a bowl and soften with a fork, then mix in the thyme and season well with salt and pepper. Butter the chicken all over with the herb butter, inside and out, and place the lemon quarters inside the body cavity. Pour the wine over the chicken.

• Roast the chicken in the centre of the oven for 20 minutes. Reduce the temperature to 190°C/375°F/Gas Mark 5 and continue to roast for a further 1¼ hours, basting frequently. Cover with foil if the skin begins to brown too much. If the tin dries out, add a little more wine or water.

• Check that the chicken is cooked by piercing the thickest part of the leg with a sharp knife or skewer and making sure the juices run clear. Remove from the oven.

• Remove the chicken from the roasting tin and place on a warmed serving plate to rest, covered with foil, for 10 minutes before carving.

• Place the roasting tin on the top of the hob and bubble the pan juices gently over a low heat until they have reduced and are thick and glossy. Season to taste with salt and pepper.

• Serve the chicken with the pan juices and scatter with the thyme sprigs.

SERVES 4

1 oven-ready goose, weighing
  3.5–4.5 kg/7 lb 12 oz–10 lb

1 tsp salt

4 pears

1 tbsp lemon juice

55 g/2 oz butter

2 tbsp clear honey

lemon slices, to garnish

seasonal vegetables, to serve

Yuletide Goose with Honey & Pears

Goose fat is simply perfect for roasting (and sautéeing) potatoes, so don't waste it. Pour any that you are not about to use immediately into a jar with a screw top and store in the refrigerator.

- Preheat the oven to 220°C/425°F/Gas Mark 7.
- Rinse the goose and pat dry. Use a fork to prick the skin all over, then rub with the salt. Place the bird upside down on a rack in a roasting tin. Roast in the oven for 30 minutes. Drain off the fat. Turn the bird over and roast for 15 minutes. Drain off the fat. Reduce the temperature to 180°C/350°F/Gas Mark 4 and roast for 15 minutes per 450 g/1 lb. Cover with foil 15 minutes before the end of the cooking time. Check that the bird is cooked by inserting a knife between the legs and body. If the juices run clear, it is cooked. Remove from the oven.
- Peel and halve the pears and brush with lemon juice. Melt the butter and honey in a saucepan over a low heat, then add the pears. Cook, stirring, for 5–10 minutes until tender. Remove from the heat, arrange the pears around the goose and pour the sweet juices over the bird. Garnish with lemon slices and serve with seasonal vegetables.

SERVES 4

5 tbsp fresh brown breadcrumbs

200 g/7 oz low-fat fromage frais

5 tbsp chopped fresh parsley

5 tbsp snipped fresh chives

4 poussins

1 tbsp sunflower oil

675 g/1 lb 8 oz young spring
  vegetables, such as carrots,

courgettes, sugar snap peas, baby
  sweetcorn and turnips, cut into
  small chunks

125 ml/4 fl oz boiling chicken stock

2 tsp cornflour

150 ml/5 fl oz dry white wine

salt and pepper

Poussins with Herbs & Wine

Poussins are simple to
prepare, quick to cook and
can be easily cut in
half lengthways with a
sharp knife.

• Preheat the oven to 220°C/425°F/Gas Mark 7.

• Mix the breadcrumbs, one third of the fromage frais and 2 tablespoons each of the parsley and chives together in a bowl. Season well with salt and pepper. Spoon into the neck ends of the poussins. Place on a rack in a roasting tin, brush with the oil and season well with salt and pepper.

• Roast in the oven for 30–35 minutes, or until the juices run clear when the thickest part of the meat is pierced with a skewer.

• Place the vegetables in a shallow ovenproof dish in a single layer and add half the remaining herbs with the stock.

• Cover and bake in the oven for 25–30 minutes until tender. Lift the poussins onto a warmed serving plate and skim any fat from the juices in the tin. Add the vegetable juices and place the tin over a medium heat.

• Blend the cornflour with the wine and whisk into the sauce with the remaining fromage frais. Whisk until boiling, then add the remaining herbs. Season to taste with salt and pepper. Spoon the sauce over the poussins and serve with the vegetables.

SERVES 6–8

1 duckling, weighing 1.8 kg/4 lb
    (dressed weight); ask your butcher
    to bone the duckling and cut off the
    wings at the first joint
450 g/1 lb flavoured sausage meat
1 small onion, finely chopped
1 Cox's apple, cored and finely
    chopped

85 g/3 oz ready-to-eat dried apricots,
    finely chopped
85 g/3 oz chopped walnuts
2 tbsp chopped fresh parsley
1 large or 2 smaller duck breasts,
    skin removed
salt and pepper

APRICOT SAUCE

400 g/14 oz canned apricot halves
150 ml/5 fl oz stock
125 ml/4 fl oz Marsala
½ tsp ground cinnamon
½ tsp ground ginger
salt and pepper

Boned & Stuffed Roast Duckling

Duckling is wonderful to serve on a special occasion, the only drawback being that there is not much meat on the bird and it can be difficult to carve. Why not have your butcher bone the duckling for you and then stuff it with good-quality sausage meat? If you add a couple of duck breasts, you can make a very substantial dish for 6–8 people that is easy to carve and looks wonderful. Serve with a sweet sauce – orange is classic, but one made with canned apricots, spiced with cinnamon and ginger, is more unusual.

• Wipe the duckling with kitchen paper both inside and out. Lay it skin-side down on a board and season well with salt and pepper.
• Mix the sausage meat, onion, apple, apricots, walnuts and parsley together. Season well with salt and pepper. Form into a large sausage shape.
• Lay the duck breast(s) on the whole duckling and cover with the stuffing. Wrap the whole duckling around the stuffing and carefully tuck in any leg and neck flaps.
• Preheat the oven to 190°C/375°F/Gas Mark 5. Sew the duckling up the back and across both ends with fine string. Try to use one piece of string so that you can remove it in one go. Mould the duckling into a good shape and place, sewn-side down, on a wire rack over a roasting tin.
• Roast in the oven for 1½–2 hours, basting occasionally. Pour off some of the fat in the tin. When it is cooked, the duckling should be golden brown and the skin crisp.
• To make the apricot sauce, purée the apricots with their syrup in a blender or food processor. Pour into a saucepan, add the stock, Marsala, cinnamon and ginger and season with salt and pepper. Stir over a low heat, then simmer for 2–3 minutes.
• Carve the duckling into thick slices at the table and serve with warm apricot sauce.

SERVES 4

1 oven-ready turkey, weighing
    5 kg/11 lb
1 garlic clove, finely chopped
100 ml/3½ fl oz red wine
75 g/2½ oz butter

STUFFING

100 g/3½ oz button mushrooms
1 onion, chopped
1 garlic clove, chopped
85 g/3 oz butter
100 g/3½ oz fresh breadcrumbs
2 tbsp finely chopped fresh sage
1 tbsp lemon juice
salt and pepper

PORT AND CRANBERRY SAUCE

100 g/3½ oz sugar
250 ml/9 fl oz port
175 g/6 oz fresh cranberries

Traditional Roast Turkey with Wine & Mushrooms

The majority of turkeys on sale are white-feathered varieties. However, the dark-feathered birds, known as bronze turkeys, are becoming increasingly popular. The skin may show the remains of dark stubble, which looks less attractive, but the flavour of bronze birds is usually superior. Norfolk Bronze and Norfolk Black are both flavoursome, plump-breasted breeds.

• Preheat the oven to 200°C/400°F/Gas Mark 6.
• To make the stuffing, clean and chop the mushrooms, put them in a saucepan with the onion, garlic and butter and cook for 3 minutes. Remove from the heat and stir in the remaining stuffing ingredients. Rinse the turkey and pat dry with kitchen paper. Fill the neck end with stuffing and truss with string.
• Put the turkey in a roasting tin. Rub the garlic over the bird and pour the wine over. Add the butter and roast in the oven for 30 minutes. Baste, then reduce the temperature to 180°C/350°F/Gas Mark 4 and roast for a further 40 minutes. Baste again and cover with foil. Roast for a further 2 hours, basting regularly. Check that the bird is cooked by inserting a knife between the legs and body. If the juices run clear, it is cooked. Remove from the oven, cover with foil and leave to stand for 25 minutes.
• Meanwhile, to make the port and cranberry sauce, put the sugar, port and cranberries in a saucepan. Heat over a medium heat until almost boiling. Reduce the heat, simmer for 15 minutes, stirring, then remove from the heat. Serve with the turkey.

SERVES 4

100 g/3½ oz butter, slightly softened

1 tbsp chopped fresh thyme

1 tbsp chopped fresh parsley

2 oven-ready young pheasants

4 tbsp vegetable oil

125 ml/4 fl oz red wine

salt and pepper

TO SERVE

honey-glazed parsnips

sautéed potatoes

freshly cooked Brussels sprouts

Roast Pheasant with Red Wine & Herbs

Only young birds are suitable for roasting, as older pheasants are fairly tough and need a slower cooking method. Even so, the meat on the legs tends to be quite tough and sinewy, whereas the lighter breasts are more delicate and tender. It is quite usual to serve only the breasts.

Keep the leg meat for making a minced pasta sauce or using in a pie. You can also make delicious stock with the carcasses.

- Preheat the oven to 190°C/375°F/Gas Mark 5.
- Put the butter in a small bowl and mix in the chopped herbs. Lift the skins off the pheasants, taking care not to tear them, and push the herb butter under the skins. Season to taste with salt and pepper. Pour the oil into a roasting tin, add the pheasants and cook in the oven for 45 minutes, basting occasionally.
- Remove from the oven, pour over the wine, then return to the oven and cook for a further 15 minutes, or until cooked through. Check that each bird is cooked by inserting a knife between the legs and body. If the juices run clear, they are cooked.
- Remove the pheasants from the oven, cover with foil and leave to stand for 15 minutes. Divide between individual serving plates, and serve with honey-glazed parsnips, sautéed potatoes and freshly cooked Brussels sprouts.

SERVES 4

1 oven-ready guinea fowl, weighing
    1.25 kg/2 lb 12 oz
½ tbsp sunflower oil
½ apple, peeled, cored and chopped
several fresh flat-leaf parsley sprigs,
    stems bruised

1 large Savoy cabbage, coarse
    outer leaves removed, cored and
    quartered
1 thick piece of smoked belly of pork,
    weighing about 140 g/5 oz, rind
    removed and cut into thin lardons,
    or 140 g/5 oz unsmoked lardons

1 onion, sliced
1 bouquet garni
1½ tbsp chopped fresh flat-leaf
    parsley
salt and pepper

Guinea Fowl with Cabbage

It is important not to add too much salt to the onion as the lardons will be salty.

• Preheat the oven to 240°C/475°F/Gas Mark 9.

• Rub the guinea fowl with the oil and season to taste inside and out with salt and pepper. Add the apple and parsley sprigs to the guinea fowl's cavity and truss to tie the legs together. Place the guinea fowl in a roasting tin and roast in the oven for 20 minutes to colour the breasts. When the guinea fowl is golden brown, reduce the oven temperature to 160°C/325°F/Gas Mark 3.

• Meanwhile, bring a large saucepan of salted water to the boil. Add the cabbage and blanch for 3 minutes. Drain, rinse in cold water and pat dry.

• Place the lardons in a flameproof casserole over a medium–high heat and sauté until they give off their fat. Use a slotted spoon to remove the lardons from the casserole and set aside.

• Add the onion to the fat left in the casserole and cook, stirring frequently, for 5 minutes, or until the onion is tender, but not brown. Stir the bouquet garni into the casserole with a very little salt and a pinch of pepper, then return the lardons to the casserole.

• Remove the guinea fowl from the oven. Add the cabbage to the casserole, top with the guinea fowl and cover the surface with a piece of wet greaseproof paper. Cover the casserole and put it in the oven for 45 minutes–1 hour, or until the guinea fowl is tender and the juices run clear when a skewer is inserted into the thickest part of the meat.

• Remove the guinea fowl from the casserole and cut into serving portions. Stir the parsley into the cabbage and onion, then taste and adjust the seasoning if necessary. Serve the guinea fowl portions on a bed of cabbage and onion.

SERVES 4

4 tbsp olive oil

8 oven-ready quail

280 g/10 oz green seedless grapes

225 ml/8 fl oz grape juice

2 cloves

about 150 ml/5 fl oz water

2 tbsp brandy

salt and pepper

POTATO PANCAKE

600 g/1 lb 5 oz unpeeled potatoes

35 g/1¼ oz unsalted butter or pork fat

1¼ tbsp olive oil

Quail with Grapes

Farmed quail, weighing 115–140 g/4–5 oz, are widely available all year round. They may be fresh or frozen and are usually oven-ready.

• Preheat the oven to 230°C/450°F/Gas Mark 8. Parboil the potatoes for the pancake in a large saucepan of lightly salted water for 10 minutes. Drain and leave to cool completely, then peel, coarsely grate and season to taste with salt and pepper. Set aside.

• Heat the oil in a heavy-based frying pan or flameproof casserole large enough to hold the quail in a single layer over a medium heat. Add the quail and fry on all sides until golden brown.

• Add the grapes, grape juice, cloves, enough water to come halfway up the sides of the quail and salt and pepper to taste. Cover and simmer for 20 minutes. Transfer the quail and all the juices to a roasting tin and sprinkle with the brandy. Place in the oven and roast, uncovered, for 10 minutes.

• Meanwhile, to make the potato pancake, melt the butter with the oil in a 30-cm/12-inch non-stick frying pan over a high heat. When the fat is hot, add the potatoes and spread into an even layer. Reduce the heat and gently cook for 10 minutes. Place a plate over the frying pan and, wearing oven gloves, invert them so that the potato pancake drops onto the plate. Slide the potato back into the frying pan and continue cooking for 10 minutes, or until cooked through and crisp. Slide out of the frying pan and cut into 4 wedges. Keep warm until the quail are ready.

• Place a potato pancake wedge and 2 quail on each plate. Taste the grape sauce and adjust the seasoning if necessary. Spoon the sauce over the quail and serve.

SERVES 4

6 tbsp vegetable oil

1.7 kg/3 lb 12 oz saddle of fresh
    venison, trimmed

salt and pepper

fresh thyme sprigs, to garnish

freshly cooked vegetables, to serve

BRANDY SAUCE

1 tbsp plain flour

4 tbsp vegetable stock

175 ml/6 fl oz brandy

100 ml/3½ fl oz double cream

Roast Venison with Brandy Sauce

Both wild and farmed venison – deer meat – are available and surprisingly inexpensive compared with lamb or beef. It may be fresh or frozen. It has a delicate texture and is high in protein, but low in fat, so it is very nutritious.

• Preheat the oven to 180°C/350°F/Gas Mark 4.

• Heat half the oil in a frying pan over a high heat. Season the venison to taste with salt and pepper, add to the pan and cook until lightly browned all over. Pour the remaining oil into a roasting pan. Add the venison, cover with foil and roast in the oven, basting occasionally, for 1½ hours, or until cooked through. Remove from the oven and transfer to a warmed serving platter. Cover with foil and set aside.

• To make the sauce, stir the flour into the roasting pan over the hob and cook for 1 minute. Pour in the stock and heat it, stirring to loosen the sediment from the base. Gradually stir in the brandy and bring to the boil, then reduce the heat and simmer, stirring, for 10–15 minutes until the sauce has thickened a little. Remove from the heat and stir in the cream.

• Garnish the venison with thyme and serve with the brandy sauce and a selection of freshly cooked vegetables.

We tend to think of roasting fish as a fairly modern technique, yet even Mrs Beeton in her famous 19th-century *Enquire Within on Household Management* includes recipes for roasting salmon, sole and mackerel, although she tends to call the process baking.

This signposts the differences between roasting meat or poultry and roasting fish. Firstly, fish cooks very much more rapidly than most meat and, secondly, its flesh is generally quite delicate and can easily be dried out by the high heat of the oven. Therefore, many recipes include extra ingredients, such as lemon or lime juice, wine, vegetables, breadcrumbs and herbs, as well as oil or butter, to protect it and keep it moist. These may be used as stuffings, crusts or sauces, or as a mixture of these.

You need to pay attention to the roasting times and to keep an eye on the fish while it is cooking, but roasting fish is not a difficult

THE OCEAN SELECTION

art and the results are simply mouth-watering. The crisp golden skin enclosing the succulent flesh of a well-roasted whole fish makes sea bass or sea bream a spectacular dinner party dish, while fillets of all kinds, whether oily or white fish, are easy to handle and serve. In particular, meaty fish with firm flesh respond well to roasting – monkfish perhaps being the best of all, although tuna runs a close second. The texture of monkfish and even its flavour have been compared – favourably – to that of roast lamb.

Seafood, such as prawns, acquires a special flavour when roasted, with the added advantage that it takes hardly any time to cook, and there is no need to stand over it and stir.

SERVES 4

1 whole sea bass, about
 1.3–1.8 kg/3–4 lb, cleaned
1 small onion, finely chopped
2 garlic cloves, finely chopped
2 tbsp finely chopped fresh herbs,
 such as parsley, chervil and
 tarragon

25 g/1 oz anchovy fillets, finely
 chopped
25 g/1 oz butter
150 ml/5 fl oz white wine
2 tbsp crème fraîche
salt and pepper

Roast Sea Bass

You can use either small individual fish to serve as single portions or one large one to share among family or friends. Individual fish, weighing 280–350 g/ 10–12 oz each, will take only 15–20 minutes to roast. Round fish like sea bass, sea bream, red mullet, red snapper, trout and mackerel are particularly good for roasting as their skin crisps up well while the flesh stays deliciously moist and creamy. Make sure you use really fresh fish if you want this dish to sparkle.

• Preheat the oven to 200°C/400°F/Gas Mark 6.

• Remove any scales from the fish and thoroughly rinse it both inside and out. If you like, trim off the fins with a pair of scissors. Using a sharp knife, make five or six cuts diagonally into the flesh of the fish on both sides. Season well with salt and pepper, both inside and out.

• Mix the onion, garlic, herbs and anchovies together in a bowl. Stuff the fish with half the mixture and spoon the remainder into a roasting tin. Place the sea bass on top. Spread the butter over the fish, pour over the wine and place in the oven. Roast for 30–35 minutes until the fish is cooked through and the flesh flakes easily.

• Using a fish slice, carefully remove the sea bass from the tin to a warmed serving platter. Place the roasting tin over a medium heat and stir the onion mixture and juices together. Add the crème fraîche, mix well and pour into a warmed serving bowl.

• Serve the sea bass whole and divide at the table. Spoon a little sauce on the side.

SERVES 4

6 tbsp extra virgin olive oil

1 onion, sliced

1 leek, sliced

juice of ½ lemon

2 tbsp chopped fresh parsley

2 tbsp chopped fresh dill

500 g/1 lb 2 oz salmon fillets

salt and pepper

freshly cooked baby spinach leaves,
   to serve

TO GARNISH

lemon slices

fresh dill sprigs

Roast Salmon with Lemon & Herbs

Although salmon is an oily fish, it has very delicate flesh that can dry out easily. Therefore, it is important to make sure that all the fillets are well coated with the oil and lemon juice mixture to protect them. Keep an eye on the fish during roasting to prevent overcooking.

• Preheat the oven to 200°C/400°F/Gas Mark 6.

• Heat 1 tablespoon of the oil in a frying pan over a medium heat. Add the onion and leek and cook, stirring occasionally, for 4 minutes, or until slightly softened.

• Meanwhile, put the remaining oil in a small bowl with the lemon juice and herbs and season to taste with salt and pepper. Stir together well. Rinse the fish under cold running water, then pat dry with kitchen paper. Arrange the fish in a shallow ovenproof dish.

• Remove the frying pan from the heat and spread the onion and leek over the fish. Pour the oil mixture over the top, making sure that everything is well coated. Roast in the centre of the preheated oven for 10 minutes, or until the fish is cooked through.

• Arrange the cooked spinach on serving plates. Remove the fish and vegetables from the oven and arrange on top of the spinach. Garnish with lemon slices and sprigs of dill. Serve immediately.

SERVES 4–6

200 ml/7 fl oz freshly squeezed
   orange juice

3 tbsp extra virgin olive oil

55 g/2 oz anchovy fillets in oil, roughly
   chopped, with the oil reserved

small pinch of dried chilli flakes,
   or to taste

1 tuna fillet, about 600 g/1 lb 5 oz

pepper

Roast Tuna with Orange & Anchovies

Just like beef, roasted tuna continues to cook after it comes out of the oven while it rests. An easy way to check whether the tuna is cooked is to insert a meat thermometer into it, through the foil, just before you put the covered tin in the oven. When the temperature reads 60°C/140°F, the tuna will be medium cooked.

• Combine the orange juice, 2 tablespoons of the olive oil, the anchovies and their oil and the chilli flakes in a non-metallic bowl large enough to hold the tuna and add pepper to taste. Add the tuna and spoon the marinade over it. Cover with clingfilm and chill in the refrigerator for at least 2 hours to marinate, turning the tuna occasionally. Remove the bowl from the refrigerator about 20 minutes before cooking to return the fish to room temperature. Meanwhile, preheat the oven to 220°C/425°F/Gas Mark 7.

• Remove the tuna from the marinade, reserving the marinade, and wipe dry. Heat the remaining oil in a large frying pan over a high heat. Add the tuna and sear for 1 minute on each side until lightly browned and crisp. Place in a small roasting tin. Cover the tin tightly with foil.

• Roast in the oven for 8 minutes for medium-rare and 10 minutes for medium-well done. Remove from the oven and set aside to rest for at least 2 minutes before slicing.

• Meanwhile, put the marinade in a small saucepan over a high heat and bring to a rolling boil. Boil for at least 2 minutes.

• Transfer the tuna to a serving platter and carve into thick slices, which will probably break into chunks as you cut them. Serve the sauce separately for spooning over. The tuna can be served hot or at room temperature, but the sauce is best hot.

SERVES 4

600 g/1 lb 5 oz new potatoes

3 red onions, cut into wedges

2 courgettes, cut into chunks

8 garlic cloves, peeled but left whole

2 lemons, cut into wedges

4 fresh rosemary sprigs

4 tbsp olive oil

350 g/12 oz unpeeled raw prawns

2 small raw squid, cut into rings

4 tomatoes, quartered

Roast Seafood

Most vegetables are suitable for roasting in the oven. Try adding 450 g/1 lb pumpkin, squash or aubergine, if you like.

- Preheat the oven to 200°C/400°F/Gas Mark 6.
- Scrub the potatoes to remove any dirt. Cut any large potatoes in half. Parboil the potatoes in a saucepan of boiling water for 10–15 minutes. Place the potatoes in a large roasting tin together with the onions, courgettes, garlic, lemons and rosemary sprigs.
- Pour over the oil and toss to coat all the vegetables in it. Roast in the oven for 30 minutes, turning occasionally, until the potatoes are tender.
- Once the potatoes are tender, add the prawns, squid and tomatoes, tossing to coat them in the oil, and roast for 10 minutes. All the vegetables should be cooked through and slightly charred for full flavour. Transfer the roast seafood and vegetables to warmed serving plates and serve hot.

SERVES 4

900 g/2 lb floury potatoes

125 ml/4 fl oz milk

55 g/2 oz butter

4 haddock fillets, about 225 g/8 oz
each

1 tbsp sunflower oil

4 garlic cloves, finely chopped

salt and pepper

2 tbsp chopped fresh parsley,
to garnish

Garlic-crusted Roast Haddock

If you prefer, you can cook the potatoes unpeeled, but do scrub them first. Peel them as soon as they are cool enough to handle, then mash as above. This helps to preserve the vitamins and minerals that lie just beneath the skin.

• Preheat the oven to 230°C/450°F/Gas Mark 8.

• Cut the potatoes into chunks and cook in a saucepan of lightly salted water for 15 minutes, or until tender. Drain well. Mash in the saucepan until smooth. Set over a low heat and beat in the milk, butter and salt and pepper to taste.

• Put the haddock fillets in a roasting tin and brush the fish with the oil. Sprinkle the garlic on top, add salt and pepper to taste, then spread with the mashed potatoes. Roast in the oven for 8–10 minutes, or until the fish is just tender.

• Meanwhile, preheat the grill. Transfer the fish to the grill and cook for about 2 minutes, or until golden brown. Sprinkle with the chopped parsley and serve immediately.

SERVES 4

250 g/9 oz dry, uncoloured
   breadcrumbs

2 tbsp milk

1 fennel bulb, thinly sliced, fronds
   reserved for garnishing

1 tbsp lemon juice

2 tbsp sambuca

1 tbsp chopped fresh thyme

1 dried bay leaf, crumbled

1 whole sea bream, about
   1.5 kg/3 lb 5 oz, cleaned, scaled
   and boned

3 tbsp olive oil, plus extra for brushing

1 red onion, chopped

300 ml/10 fl oz dry white wine

salt and pepper

lemon wedges, to serve

Roast Sea Bream with Fennel

Sambuca is an Italian liqueur distilled from witch elder, but it has a strong aniseed flavour, which marries well with fish. If it is unavailable, substitute Pernod.

• Preheat the oven to 240°C/475°F/Gas Mark 9.

• Place the breadcrumbs in a bowl, add the milk and set aside for 5 minutes to soak. Place the fennel in another bowl and add the lemon juice, sambuca, thyme and bay leaf. Squeeze the breadcrumbs and add them to the fennel mixture, stirring well.

• Rinse the fish inside and out under cold running water and pat dry with kitchen paper. Season to taste with salt and pepper. Spoon the fennel mixture into the cavity, then bind the fish with trussing thread or kitchen string.

• Brush a large ovenproof dish with oil and sprinkle the onion over the base. Lay the fish on top and pour in the wine – it should reach about one third of the way up the fish. Drizzle the fish with the oil and roast in the oven for 25–30 minutes. Baste the fish occasionally with the cooking juices, and if it begins to brown, cover with a piece of foil to protect it.

• Carefully lift out the sea bream with a fish slice, remove the string and place on a warmed serving platter. Garnish with the reserved fennel fronds and serve immediately with lemon wedges for squeezing over the fish.

SERVES 4

25 g/1 oz butter

50 g/1¾ oz fresh wholemeal
    breadcrumbs

25 g/1 oz chopped walnuts

grated rind and juice of 2 lemons

2 fresh rosemary sprigs, stalks
    removed

2 tbsp chopped fresh parsley

4 cod fillets, about 150 g/5½ oz each

1 garlic clove, crushed

1 small fresh red chilli, diced

3 tbsp walnut oil

mixed salad leaves, to serve

Italian Cod

If preferred, the walnuts may be omitted from the crust. In addition, extra virgin olive oil can be used instead of walnut oil, if you like.

- Preheat the oven to 200°C/400°F/Gas Mark 6.
- Melt the butter in a large saucepan over a low heat, stirring constantly. Remove the pan from the heat and add the breadcrumbs, walnuts, the rind and juice of 1 lemon, half the rosemary and half the parsley, stirring to mix. Press the breadcrumb mixture over the top of the cod fillets. Place the cod fillets in a shallow foil-lined roasting tin. Roast the fish in the oven for 25–30 minutes.
- Mix the garlic, the remaining lemon rind and juice, rosemary, parsley and the chilli together in a bowl. Beat in the oil and mix to combine. Drizzle the dressing over the cod steaks as soon as they are cooked.
- Transfer the fish to warmed serving plates and serve immediately with salad leaves.

SERVES 4

4 tbsp basil oil or extra virgin olive oil

2 garlic cloves, chopped

1 onion, sliced

2 courgettes, sliced

6 plum tomatoes, sliced

12 black olives, stoned and halved

1 tbsp tomato purée

4 tbsp red wine

100 ml/3½ fl oz fish stock

2 tbsp chopped fresh parsley

2 tbsp chopped fresh basil

4 large mackerel, cleaned

salt and pepper

lemon slices and fresh basil sprigs,
    to garnish

freshly cooked spaghetti, salad leaves
    and spring onions, to serve

Roasted Mackerel Mediterranean-Style

The Mediterranean diet is said to be among the healthiest – this dish is a perfect example. Mackerel provides essential fatty acids, olive oil is high in vitamin A and monounsaturated ('good') fats, while tomatoes, especially cooked ones, have many health-enhancing properties.

- Preheat the oven to 200°C/400°F/Gas Mark 6.
- Heat 1 tablespoon of the oil in a large frying pan over a medium heat. Add the garlic, onion and courgettes and cook, stirring occasionally, for 4 minutes. Add the tomatoes, olives, tomato purée, wine, stock, herbs and salt and pepper to taste. Bring to the boil, then reduce the heat to medium. Cook, stirring frequently, for 10 minutes.
- Rinse the fish under cold running water, then pat dry with kitchen paper. Arrange the fish in a shallow ovenproof dish and drizzle the remaining oil over. Remove the frying pan from the heat and spread the tomato sauce over the fish. Roast the fish in the centre of the preheated oven for 10 minutes, or until they are cooked through.
- Remove from the oven, arrange the fish in their sauce on plates of freshly cooked spaghetti and garnish with lemon slices and sprigs of basil. Serve accompanied by a side salad of salad leaves and spring onions.

SERVES 4

1 kg/2 lb 4 oz white fish fillets, such
　　as bass, plaice or cod

1 lime, halved

3 tbsp extra virgin olive oil

1 large onion, finely chopped

3 garlic cloves, finely chopped

2–3 pickled jalapeño chillies
　　(jalapeños en escabeche), chopped

6–8 tbsp chopped fresh coriander

salt and pepper

lemon and lime wedges, to serve

Fish Roasted with Lime

Tangy and simple to
prepare, this is excellent
served with rice and beans
for an easy lunch – serve
with a glass of chilled beer.

• Preheat the oven to 180°C/350°F/Gas Mark 4.

• Place the fish fillets in a non-metallic bowl and season to taste with salt and pepper. Squeeze the juice from the lime halves over the fish.

• Heat the oil in a frying pan. Add the onion and garlic and cook, stirring frequently, for 2 minutes, or until softened. Remove the frying pan from the heat.

• Place a third of the onion mixture and a little of the chillies and coriander in the base of a shallow ovenproof dish or roasting tin. Arrange the fish on top. Top with the remaining onion mixture, chillies and coriander.

• Roast in the oven for 15–20 minutes, or until the fish has become slightly opaque and firm to the touch. Serve immediately, with lemon and lime wedges for squeezing over the fish.

No book about roasting food would be complete without roast potatoes, the perfect partner for roast meat and poultry. The many fans of this vegetable will be delighted to discover that there is more than one way to enjoy this superb accompaniment to a wide variety of dishes. Roast potatoes, served hot or cold, also make the most delicious snacks when sprinkled with salt and eaten with the fingers.

Other vegetables also lend themselves to this method of cooking. Roasting brings out the full flavour and a delightful sweetness in many root vegetables, such as carrots, parsnips, turnips and sweet potatoes. Squashes, from butternuts to courgettes, and Mediterranean vegetables, such as tomatoes, aubergines and peppers, make wonderful medleys that can be served as a vegetarian main course or as a side dish.

FRESH FROM THE GARDEN

Other vegetables, from onions to fennel, work well on their own. Roasting not only develops a succulent depth of flavour, but often also creates an unusual crisp texture.

Serving roast vegetables, as a colourful mix or as individual high notes, with roast meat, poultry, game or fish makes economic sense, too. If the oven will be switched on anyway, why not make full use of the space available? This helps save the housekeeping budget and uses fewer fuel resources. It also makes preparing a meal for family or guests almost trouble-free, as roasting rarely requires a lot of attention and time in the kitchen. Mix and match the recipes from earlier chapters with those in this one, keeping an eye open for compatible oven temperatures and checking cooking times.

SERVES 6

1.3 kg/3 lb large floury potatoes,
     such as King Edwards, Maris Piper
     or Desirée, peeled and cut into
     even-sized chunks
3 tbsp dripping, goose fat, duck fat or
     olive oil
salt

Perfect Roast Potatoes

Perfect roast potatoes are crisp on the outside and soft and fluffy on the inside. Do choose the right potatoes – floury ones are best. The choice of fat is also important – goose or duck fat gives an amazing flavour.

- Preheat the oven to 220°C/425°F/Gas Mark 7.
- Cook the potatoes in a large saucepan of lightly salted boiling water over a medium heat, covered, for 5–7 minutes. They will still be firm. Remove from the heat. Meanwhile, add the fat to a roasting tin and place in the hot oven.
- Drain the potatoes well and return them to the saucepan. Cover with the lid and firmly shake the pan so that the surface of the potatoes is slightly roughened to help give a much crisper texture. Remove the roasting tin from the oven and carefully tip the potatoes into the hot fat. Baste them to ensure that they are all coated with it.
- Roast the potatoes at the top of the oven for 45–50 minutes until they are browned all over and thoroughly crisp. Turn the potatoes and baste again only once during the process or the crunchy edges will be destroyed.
- Using a slotted spoon, carefully transfer the potatoes from the roasting tin into a warmed serving dish. Sprinkle with a little salt and serve immediately. Any leftovers (although this is most unlikely) are delicious cold.

SERVES 4

2 whole garlic bulbs

1 tbsp olive oil

900 g/2 lb floury potatoes, peeled

125 ml/4 fl oz milk

55 g/2 oz butter

salt and pepper

Roasted Garlic Mashed Potatoes

When roasted, garlic loses its pungent acidity and acquires a delicious, full-flavoured sweetness. So although using two whole bulbs may seem excessive, you will be surprised at the uniquely mellow flavour. In addition, roasted garlic leaves very little trace of its smell on the breath.

• Preheat the oven to 180°C/350°F/Gas Mark 4. Separate the garlic cloves, place on a large piece of foil and drizzle with the oil. Wrap the garlic in the foil and roast in the oven for about 1 hour, or until very tender. Leave to cool slightly.

• Twenty minutes before the end of the cooking time, cut the potatoes into chunks, then cook in a saucepan of lightly salted boiling water for 15 minutes, or until tender.

• Meanwhile, squeeze the cooled garlic cloves out of their skins and push through a sieve into a saucepan. Add the milk, butter and salt and pepper to taste and gently heat until the butter has melted.

• Drain the cooked potatoes, then mash in the saucepan until smooth. Pour in the garlic mixture and gently heat, stirring, until the ingredients are combined. Serve hot.

SERVES 4

500 g/1 lb 2 oz small new potatoes,
    scrubbed

150 ml/5 fl oz vegetable oil

1 tsp chilli powder

½ tsp caraway seeds

1 tsp salt

Chilli Roast Potatoes

For this delicious side dish, small new potatoes are scrubbed and boiled in their skins, before being coated in a hot chilli mixture and roasted to perfection in the oven.

• Preheat the oven to 200°C/400°F/Gas Mark 6. Cook the potatoes in a large saucepan of boiling water for 10 minutes, then thoroughly drain.

• Meanwhile, pour a little of the oil into a shallow roasting tin to coat the base. Heat the oil in the oven for 10 minutes, then remove the tin from the oven. Add the potatoes and brush them with the hot oil.

• Mix the chilli powder, caraway seeds and salt together in a small bowl, then evenly sprinkle the mixture over the potatoes, turning them to coat. Add the remaining oil to the tin and return to the oven to roast for 15 minutes, or until the potatoes are cooked through and golden brown.

• Using a slotted spoon, remove the potatoes from the tin, draining well, transfer to a large warmed serving dish and serve immediately.

SERVES 4–6

3 parsnips, cut into 5-cm/2-inch
    chunks
4 baby turnips, quartered
3 carrots, cut into 5-cm/2-inch chunks
450 g/1 lb butternut squash, peeled
    and cut into 5-cm/2-inch chunks
450 g/1 lb sweet potatoes, peeled
    and cut into 5-cm/2-inch chunks

2 garlic cloves, finely chopped
2 tbsp chopped fresh rosemary
2 tbsp chopped fresh thyme
2 tsp chopped fresh sage
3 tbsp olive oil
salt and pepper
2 tbsp chopped fresh mixed herbs,
    such as parsley, thyme and mint,
    to garnish

Roast Root Vegetables

Root vegetables are our winter staples. Roast root vegetables are particularly popular since they all cook together and need little attention once prepared. You can use whatever is available: potatoes, parsnips, turnips, swedes, carrots and, although not strictly root vegetables, squash and onions.

• Preheat the oven to 220°C/425°F/Gas Mark 7.
• Arrange all the vegetables in a single layer in a large roasting tin. Scatter over the garlic and the herbs. Pour over the oil and season well with salt and pepper.
• Toss all the ingredients together until they are well mixed and coated with the oil (you can leave them to marinate at this stage to allow the flavours to be absorbed).
• Roast the vegetables at the top of the oven for 30–45 minutes until they are cooked and nicely browned. Turn the vegetables over halfway through the cooking time.
• Serve with a good handful of fresh herbs scattered on top and a final sprinkling of salt and pepper to taste.

SERVES 4

2 tbsp olive oil

1 fennel bulb

2 red onions

2 beef tomatoes

1 aubergine

2 courgettes

1 yellow pepper

1 red pepper

1 orange pepper

4 garlic cloves, peeled but left whole

4 fresh rosemary sprigs

pepper

crusty bread, to serve (optional)

Roast Summer Vegetables

This appetizing and colourful mixture of Mediterranean vegetables makes a sensational summer lunch for vegetarians and meat-eaters alike. Roasting brings out the full flavour and sweetness of the peppers, aubergines, courgettes and onions.

• Preheat the oven to 200°C/400°F/Gas Mark 6.

• Brush a large ovenproof dish with a little of the oil. Prepare the vegetables. Cut the fennel bulb, red onions and tomatoes into wedges. Thickly slice the aubergine and courgettes, then deseed all the peppers and cut into chunks. Arrange the vegetables in the dish and tuck the garlic cloves and rosemary sprigs between them. Drizzle with the remaining oil and season to taste with pepper.

• Roast the vegetables in the oven for 10 minutes. Remove the dish from the oven and turn over the vegetables using a slotted spoon. Return the dish to the oven and roast for a further 10–15 minutes, or until the vegetables are tender and beginning to turn golden brown.

• Serve the vegetables straight from the dish or transfer them to a warmed serving plate. For a vegetarian main course, serve with crusty bread, if you like.

SERVES 4

8 large onions, peeled but left whole

3 tbsp olive oil

55 g/2 oz butter

2 tsp chopped fresh thyme

200 g/7 oz Cheddar or Lancashire
cheese, grated

salt and pepper

salad and warm crusty bread, to serve

Roast Onions

For stuffed onions, boil 4 peeled onions in salted water for 20 minutes. Scoop out the centres with a teaspoon and stuff with a mixture of 55 g/2 oz grated cheese, 55 g/2 oz breadcrumbs and 1 teaspoon mustard. Place the onions in an ovenproof dish, dot with 25 g/1 oz butter and roast in a preheated oven, 220°C/425°F/Gas Mark 7, for 25–30 minutes. Serve hot as a starter or as an accompaniment to roast meat.

- Preheat the oven to 180°C/350°F/Gas Mark 4.
- Cut a cross down through the top of each onion towards the root, without cutting all the way through. Place the onions in a roasting tin and drizzle over the oil.
- Press a little of the butter into the open crosses, sprinkle with the thyme and season to taste with salt and pepper. Cover with foil and roast in the oven for 40–45 minutes.
- Remove the tin from the oven, take off and discard the foil and baste the onions with the pan juices. Return to the oven and cook for a further 15 minutes, uncovered, to allow the onions to brown.
- Take the onions out of the oven and scatter the grated cheese over them. Return them to the oven for a few minutes so that the cheese starts to melt.
- Serve immediately with some salad and lots of warm crusty bread.

SERVES 4

450 g/1 lb asparagus spears

2 tbsp extra virgin olive oil

1 tsp coarse sea salt

1 tbsp freshly grated Parmesan
cheese, to serve

Crispy Roast Asparagus

As well as there being both green and white varieties of asparagus, there is considerable variation in width, so it is important to try to find spears of a similar size. Otherwise, some will be tender while others require further cooking. As a general rule, the stems of green asparagus rarely need peeling, but those of white asparagus do.

• Preheat the oven to 200°C/400°F/Gas Mark 6.

• Choose asparagus spears of similar widths. Trim the base of the spears so that all the stems are approximately the same length.

• Arrange the asparagus in a single layer on a baking sheet. Drizzle with the oil and sprinkle with the salt.

• Place the baking sheet in the oven and roast the asparagus for 10–15 minutes, turning the spears once. Remove from the oven and transfer to a warmed dish. Serve immediately, sprinkled with grated Parmesan cheese.

SERVES 6

4 leeks

3 tbsp olive oil

2 tsp balsamic vinegar

sea salt and pepper

Roast Leeks

If in season, 8 baby leeks may be used instead of the standard-sized ones. Sherry vinegar makes a good substitute for the expensive balsamic vinegar and would work as well in this recipe.

• Preheat the oven to 200°C/400°F/Gas Mark 6.

• Halve the leeks lengthways, making sure that your knife cuts straight, so that the leek is held together by the root. Thoroughly rinse the leeks, gently fanning the layers, under cold running water to remove all traces of soil and grit. Pat dry with kitchen paper.

• Cut off the roots, place the leek halves in a roasting tin and brush with the oil. Roast in the oven for 20–30 minutes until tender and just beginning to colour.

• Remove the leeks from the oven and brush with balsamic vinegar. Sprinkle with salt and pepper to taste and serve hot or warm.

There is nothing to match the flavour of a cookie that has been freshly baked that day. So simple to make, yet so satisfying to eat, cookies and bars are quite simply the most indulgent treat for children and adults alike. They are the perfect way to round off a lunch or dinner or to serve as a mid-morning treat. Try serving with an interesting variety of tea or a special brand of coffee for an indulgent treat. Make a batch in a quiet moment and you'll have something special to hand for when the family comes home or friends call round unexpectedly. They are also the perfect after-school treat for hungry kids – in moderation, of course!

Baking biscuits in your own kitchen is immensely satisfying (in fact, some don't even require baking). A huge bonus is the wonderful aroma that will fill your house as your creations cook – and the smell

family favourites, such as brownies and flapjacks, to delicate morsels, such as Florentines and Amaretti, you will be spoilt for choice. Among all these cookies and bars you are sure to find at least one that is perfect for morning coffee, afternoon tea, school lunch boxes, or serving with ice cream for dessert. Or for an extra special home-made gift, treat friends and family to a selection of cookies in a pretty box or cellophane bag tied with ribbon. The personal touch is always appreciated.

There is no specialist equipment required – just a few sturdy baking sheets and a wire rack to allow your creations to cool. A pallet knife will come in useful to lift cookies off baking sheets, but this is not essential. Armed with the following recipes, your kitchen will soon become a veritable feast of delicious home-baked treats.

INTRODUCTION TO
COOKIES & BARS

of home-baking creates a wonderful impression for would-be buyers if your house is on the market! In addition, they're easy to make and take very little time, so you can whisk up a batch of tasty treats in no time at all. You can even encourage the kids – major consumers of cookies and bars, after all – to help mix dough and cut it out. This could be a constructive and fun rainy-day pastime.

The recipes are divided into four chapters which are chock-full with fabulous ideas for cookies and bars, including chocolate cookies, fruity bites and nut-based morsels. There is also a chapter on the most exotic cookies you could wish to make for special occasions. From

Perennially popular with adults and children alike, chocolate biscuits, brownies and bars are, arguably, everybody's favourite sweet treat. Certainly, chocoholics will not be disappointed by the fabulous collection of recipes in this chapter, which includes everything from what might be described as the best biscuits in the world – Double Chocolate Chip Cookies – to mouth-watering Caramel Chocolate Shortbread.

Cooking with chocolate is not difficult but it does require a little care. To blend chocolate with other ingredients, it usually needs to be melted. The easiest way to do this is to break it into small pieces and place them in a heatproof bowl. Set the bowl over a pan of gently simmering, not boiling, water and heat until the chocolate has melted. Do not let the base of the bowl touch the surface of

CHOCOLATE HEAVEN

the water and make sure that, if you are stirring the chocolate or a mixture of chocolate and other ingredients, water does not splash into the bowl because it will make the chocolate grainy and spoil the texture of the biscuit or its chocolate topping. You can also melt chocolate in the microwave. Break it into pieces and arrange in a microwave dish. Check with the manufacturer's handbook for timings, bearing in mind that white chocolate should be melted on medium, while plain or milk chocolate can be melted on high. Remove the dish and stir frequently to check whether the chocolate has melted. Chocolate can be melted over direct heat in a saucepan if it is combined with one or more ingredients, such as butter and syrup.

MAKES 20

115 g/4 oz unsalted butter, softened,
   plus extra for greasing

55 g/2 oz golden granulated sugar

55 g/2 oz light muscovado sugar

1 egg, beaten

½ tsp vanilla essence

115 g/4 oz plain flour

2 tbsp cocoa powder

½ tsp bicarbonate of soda

115 g/4 oz milk chocolate chips

55 g/2 oz walnuts, roughly chopped

Double Chocolate Chip Cookies

The minimum cooking time will produce cookies that are soft and chewy in the middle. The longer cooking time will result in crisper cookies.

• Preheat the oven to 180°C/350°F/Gas Mark 4, then grease 3 baking sheets. Place the butter, granulated sugar and muscovado sugar in a bowl and beat until light and fluffy. Gradually beat in the egg and vanilla essence.

• Sift the flour, cocoa and bicarbonate of soda into the mixture and stir in carefully. Stir in the chocolate chips and walnuts. Drop dessertspoonfuls of the mixture on to the prepared baking sheets, spaced well apart to allow for spreading.

• Bake in the oven for 10–15 minutes, or until the mixture has spread and the cookies are beginning to feel firm.

• Remove from the oven, leave on the baking sheets for 2 minutes, then transfer to wire racks to cool completely.

MAKES 24

175 g/6 oz unsalted butter or
   margarine, plus extra for greasing

200 g/7 oz soft brown sugar

1 egg

70 g/2½ oz plain flour

1 tsp bicarbonate of soda

pinch of salt

70 g/2½ oz wholemeal flour

1 tbsp bran

225 g/8 oz plain chocolate chips

185 g/6½ oz rolled oats

1 tbsp strong coffee

100 g/3½ oz hazelnuts, toasted and
   chopped roughly

Chocolate and Coffee Wholemeal Cookies

These delicious dark
biscuits, flavoured with
coffee and toasted chopped
hazelnuts, are perfect
served with coffee.

• Preheat the oven to 190°C/375°F/Gas Mark 5. Grease 2 large baking sheets. Cream the butter and sugar together in a bowl. Add the egg and beat well, using a hand whisk if preferred.

• In a separate bowl, sift together the plain flour, bicarbonate of soda and salt, then add in the wholemeal flour and bran. Mix in the egg mixture, then stir in the chocolate chips, oats, coffee and hazelnuts. Mix well, with an electric whisk if preferred.

• Put 24 rounded tablespoonfuls of the mixture on to the prepared baking sheets, allowing room for the biscuits to spread during cooking. Alternatively, with lightly floured hands, break off pieces of the mixture and roll into balls (about 25 g/1 oz each), place on the baking sheets and flatten them with the back of a teaspoon. Transfer the baking sheets to the preheated oven and bake for 16–18 minutes, or until the biscuits are golden brown.

• Remove from the oven, transfer the biscuits to a wire rack and leave to cool before serving.

MAKES 18–20

55 g/2 oz plain chocolate, broken
   into pieces

140 g/5 oz plain flour

1 tsp baking powder

1 egg

140 g/5 oz caster sugar

50 ml/2 fl oz sunflower oil,
   plus extra for oiling

½ tsp vanilla essence

2 tbsp icing sugar

1 small packet milk chocolate buttons
   (about 30 buttons)

1 small packet white chocolate
   buttons (about 30 buttons)

Zebra Cookies

These biscuits are topped with milk chocolate and white chocolate buttons, making them a favourite with children. Leave to cool completely before serving.

- Melt the plain chocolate in a heatproof bowl set over a saucepan of gently simmering water. Remove from the heat and leave to cool. Sift the flour and baking powder together.
- Meanwhile, in a large bowl, whisk the egg, sugar, oil and vanilla essence together. Whisk in the cooled, melted chocolate until well blended, then gradually stir in the flour. Cover the bowl with clingfilm and refrigerate for at least 3 hours.
- Preheat the oven to 190°C/375°F/Gas Mark 5. Oil 1–2 large baking sheets. Shape tablespoonfuls of the mixture into log shapes using your hands, each measuring about 5 cm/2 inches. Generously roll the logs in the icing sugar, then place on the prepared baking sheets, allowing room for the biscuits to spread during cooking.
- Bake the biscuits in the preheated oven for about 15 minutes, until firm. Remove from the oven, and place 3 chocolate buttons down the centre of each, alternating the colours. Transfer to a wire rack and leave to cool.

MAKES 20

115 g/4 oz unsalted butter, softened,
    plus extra for greasing
115 g/4 oz light muscovado sugar
1 egg
100 g/3½ oz porridge oats
1 tbsp milk
1 tsp vanilla essence

125 g/4½ oz plain flour
1 tbsp cocoa powder
½ tsp baking powder
175 g/6 oz plain chocolate, broken into
    pieces
175 g/6 oz milk chocolate,
    broken into pieces

Chocolate Chip Oaties

After baking, biscuits must be left on the baking sheet for 2 minutes, because this ensures they do not fall apart when transferred to a wire rack to cool.

• Preheat the oven to 180°C/350°F/Gas Mark 4. Grease 2 large baking sheets. Place the butter and sugar in a bowl and beat together with a wooden spoon until light and fluffy.

• Beat in the egg, then add the oats, milk and vanilla essence. Beat together until well blended. Sift the flour, cocoa and baking powder into the mixture and stir. Stir in the chocolate pieces.

• Place dessertspoonfuls of the mixture on the prepared baking sheets and flatten slightly with a fork. Bake in the preheated oven for 15 minutes, or until slightly risen and firm. Remove from the oven, cool on the baking sheets for 2 minutes, then transfer to wire racks to cool completely.

MAKES 24

90 g/3¼ oz unsalted butter, plus extra
   for greasing

365 g/12½ oz plain chocolate

1 tsp strong coffee

2 eggs

140 g/5 oz soft brown sugar

185 g/6½ oz plain flour

¼ tsp baking powder

pinch of salt

2 tsp almond essence

85 g/3 oz Brazil nuts, chopped

85 g/3 oz hazelnuts, chopped

40 g/1½ oz white chocolate

Chocolate Temptations

Piping white and dark chocolate lines over these biscuits gives them a touch of elegance and sophistication.

• Preheat the oven to 180°C/350°F/Gas Mark 4. Grease 1–2 large baking sheets. Put 225 g/8 oz of the plain chocolate with the butter and coffee into a heatproof bowl set over a saucepan of gently simmering water and heat until the chocolate is almost melted.

• Meanwhile, beat the eggs in a bowl until fluffy. Gradually whisk in the sugar until thick. Remove the chocolate from the heat and stir until smooth. Add to the egg mixture and stir until combined.

• Sift the flour, baking powder and salt into a bowl, then stir into the chocolate mixture. Chop 85 g/3 oz of the remaining plain chocolate into pieces and stir into the mixture. Stir in the almond essence and chopped nuts.

• Put 24 tablespoonfuls of the mixture on to the baking sheet, transfer to the preheated oven and bake for 16 minutes. Remove from the oven and transfer to a wire rack to cool. To decorate, melt the remaining chocolate (plain and white) in turn as in step 1, then spoon into a piping bag and pipe thin lines on to the biscuits.

MAKES 9

75 g/2¾ oz unsalted butter or
　margarine, plus extra for greasing
225 g/8 oz plain chocolate digestive
　biscuits
200 ml/7 fl oz canned evaporated milk

1 egg, beaten
1 tsp vanilla essence
2 tbsp caster sugar
40 g/1½ oz self-raising flour, sieved
125 g/4½ oz grated coconut
50 g/1¾ oz plain chocolate (optional)

Chocolate Coconut Layers

You can store the squares in an airtight container for up to 4 days. They can be frozen, undecorated, for up to 2 months. Defrost at room temperature.

• Preheat the oven to 190°C/375°F/Gas Mark 5. Grease a shallow 20-cm/8-inch square cake tin and line the bottom with baking paper.
• Crush the biscuits in a polythene bag with a rolling pin or process them in a food processor. Melt the butter in a saucepan and thoroughly stir in the crushed biscuits. Remove from the heat and press the mixture into the bottom of the prepared cake tin.
• In a separate bowl, beat the evaporated milk, egg, vanilla and sugar together until smooth. Stir in the flour and grated coconut. Pour over the biscuit layer and use a palette knife to smooth the top.
• Bake in the preheated oven for 30 minutes, or until the coconut topping has become firm and just golden. Remove from the oven, leave to cool in the tin for about 5 minutes, then cut into squares. Leave to cool completely in the tin.
• Carefully remove the squares from the tin and place them on a chopping board. Melt the plain chocolate (if using) and drizzle it over the squares to decorate them. Leave the chocolate to set before serving.

MAKES 9

115 g/4 oz unsalted butter, plus extra
for greasing

225 g/8 oz white chocolate

75 g/2¾ oz walnut pieces

2 eggs

115 g/4 oz soft brown sugar

115 g/4 oz self-raising flour

White Chocolate Brownies

You can vary the nuts in this recipe by using almonds, pecans or hazelnuts instead of the walnuts.

- Preheat the oven to 180°C/350°F/Gas Mark 4. Lightly grease an 18-cm/7-inch square cake tin.
- Coarsely chop 6 squares of white chocolate and all the walnuts. Put the remaining chocolate and the butter in a heatproof bowl set over a pan of gently simmering water. When melted, stir together, then set aside to cool slightly.
- Whisk the eggs and sugar together, then beat in the cooled chocolate mixture until well mixed. Fold in the flour, chopped chocolate and the walnuts. Turn the mixture into the prepared tin and smooth the surface.
- Transfer the tin to the preheated oven and bake for about 30 minutes, until just set. The mixture should still be a little soft in the centre. Remove from the oven, leave to cool in the tin, then cut into 9 squares before serving.

MAKES 20

85 g/3 oz unsalted butter, plus extra
for greasing

100 g/3½ oz demerara sugar

1 egg

25 g/1 oz wheatgerm

125 g/4½ oz wholemeal self-raising
flour

6 tbsp self-raising flour, sifted

125 g/4½ oz plain chocolate, broken
into pieces

Chocolate Wheatmeals

These biscuits can be frozen very successfully. Freeze them after they have cooled completely but before dipping in the melted chocolate. Thaw, dip them in melted chocolate, then leave to set before serving.

• Preheat the oven to 180°C/350°F/Gas Mark 4. Grease 1–2 baking sheets. Beat the butter and sugar in a bowl until fluffy. Add the egg and beat well. Stir in the wheatgerm and flours. Bring the mixture together with your hands.

• Roll rounded teaspoons of the mixture into balls and place on the prepared baking sheet or sheets, spaced well apart to allow for spreading. Flatten the biscuits slightly with a fork, then bake in the preheated oven for 15–20 minutes, or until golden.

• Remove from the oven and leave to cool on the baking sheets for a few minutes before transferring to a wire rack to cool completely.

• Melt the chocolate in a heatproof bowl set over a saucepan of gently simmering water, then dip each biscuit in the chocolate to cover the base and a little way up the sides. Let the excess chocolate drip back into the bowl. Place the biscuits on a sheet of baking paper and leave to set in a cool place before serving.

MAKES 12

115 g/4 oz unsalted butter, plus extra
    for greasing
175 g/6 oz plain flour
55 g/2 oz golden caster sugar

FILLING AND TOPPING

175 g/6 oz butter
115 g/4 oz golden caster sugar
3 tbsp golden syrup
400 ml/14 fl oz canned condensed
    milk
200 g/7 oz plain chocolate, broken
    into pieces

Caramel Chocolate Shortbread

Take great care when cooking the caramel filling because it can very easily catch and burn on the base of the saucepan. Stir the mixture constantly until it has thickened.

• Preheat the oven to 180°C/350°F/Gas Mark 4. Grease and line the base of a 23-cm/9-inch shallow square cake tin. Place the butter, flour and sugar in a food processor and process until they begin to bind together. Press the mixture into the prepared tin and smooth the top. Bake in the preheated oven for 20–25 minutes, or until golden.

• Meanwhile, make the filling. Place the butter, sugar, syrup and condensed milk in a saucepan and gently heat until the sugar has dissolved. Bring to the boil and simmer for 6–8 minutes, stirring constantly, until the mixture becomes very thick. Remove the shortbread base from the oven, pour over the filling and chill in the refrigerator until firm.

• To make the topping, melt the chocolate in a heatproof bowl set over a saucepan of gently simmering water. Remove from the heat, leave to cool slightly, then spread over the caramel. Chill in the refrigerator until set. Cut it into 12 pieces with a sharp knife and serve.

Nuts are positive powerhouses of energy, so when you need a pick-me-up, whether with a well-earned morning mug of coffee or a restorative cup of tea in the afternoon, this chapter is packed with just what the doctor ordered. The cookies and bars in this chapter are great in lunch boxes for the children, too — especially because with homemade cookies, you choose just how much sugar and salt you want to include. A pecan cookie or a bar of hazelnut crunch, served with a glass of milk or fruit juice, will also satisfy after-school hunger pangs. In this chapter almonds, hazelnuts, pecans and walnuts are matched with tasty combinations of oats, spices, chocolate, syrup, fruit and even coffee to produce delicious nibbles for any time of day when you fancy a nourishing snack. And what could be nicer than homemade cookies served with dessert at the end of a dinner party?

NUTTY BUT NICE

Nuts have a short storage life and can turn rancid very rapidly. Therefore it is best to buy them in fairly small quantities, as and when you need them, and store them in airtight containers in a cool, dark place. In any case, keep an eye on the 'use by' date on the packaging. For best results, buy nuts in their shells and crack them open when you want to use them. Although this is time-consuming, the flavour and texture will be much better than using ready-shelled nuts. Discard any nuts with signs of mould on the shells or kernels, for not only will these taste horrible, spoiling all your hard work, they may contain toxins, which can cause unpleasant or even serious illness.

MAKES 9

115 g/4 oz unsalted butter, plus extra
    for greasing

225 g/8 oz soft brown sugar

1 egg

1 egg yolk

140 g/5 oz self-raising flour

1 tsp ground cinnamon

85 g/3 oz walnuts, roughly chopped

Walnut & Cinnamon Blondies

Do not chop the walnuts too finely, because the blondies should have a good texture and a slight crunch to them.

• Preheat the oven to 180°C/350°F/Gas Mark 4. Grease and line the base and sides of an 18-cm/7-inch square cake tin. Place the butter and sugar in a saucepan over a low heat and stir until the sugar has dissolved. Cook, stirring, for 1 minute more. The mixture will bubble slightly, but do not let it boil. Leave to cool for 10 minutes.

• Stir the egg and egg yolk into the mixture. Sift in the flour and cinnamon, then add the nuts and stir until just blended. Pour the cake mixture into the prepared pan and bake in the preheated oven for 20–25 minutes, or until springy in the middle and a toothpick inserted into the centre comes out clean.

• Leave to cool in the tin for a few minutes, then run a knife around the edge of the tin to loosen. Turn out on to a wire rack and peel off the paper. Leave to cool completely. When cold, cut into squares.

MAKES 15

115 g/4 oz unsalted butter, softened,
    plus extra for greasing
85 g/3 oz light muscovado sugar
1 egg, beaten

55 g/2 oz pecan nuts, chopped
85 g/3 oz plain flour
½ tsp baking powder
55 g/2 oz porridge oats

Oatie Pecan Cookies

To save a lot of hard work, beat the butter and sugar together with an electric hand-held mixer. Alternatively, use a food processor.

• Preheat the oven to 180°C/350°F/Gas Mark 4, then grease 2 baking sheets. Place the butter and sugar in a bowl and beat until light and fluffy. Gradually beat in the egg, then stir in the nuts.

• Sift the flour and baking powder into the mixture and add the oats. Stir together until well combined. Drop dessertspoonfuls of the mixture on to the prepared baking sheets, spaced well apart to allow for spreading.

• Bake in the preheated oven for 15 minutes, or until pale golden. Remove from the oven, leave to cool on the baking sheets for 2 minutes, then transfer to wire racks to cool completely.

MAKES 8

3 eggs

60 g/2¼ oz ground almonds

140 g/5 oz milk powder

200 g/7 oz granulated sugar

½ tsp saffron threads

115 g/4 oz unsalted butter

1 tbsp flaked almonds, to decorate

Almond Slices

These almond slices are best eaten hot, but they may also be served cold. They can be made a day or even a week in advance and reheated. They also freeze beautifully.

• Preheat the oven to 160°C/325°F/Gas Mark 3. Lightly beat the eggs together in a mixing bowl and set aside.

• Place the ground almonds, milk powder, sugar and saffron in a large mixing bowl and stir to mix well.

• Melt the butter in a small saucepan over a low heat. Pour the melted butter over the dry ingredients and mix well with a wooden spoon until thoroughly combined.

• Add the beaten eggs to the mixture and stir to blend well.

• Evenly spread the mixture in a shallow 20-cm/8-inch ovenproof dish and bake in the preheated oven for 45 minutes, or until a cocktail stick inserted into the centre comes out clean.

• Remove from the oven and cut into slices. Decorate the slices with slivered almonds and transfer to serving plates. Serve hot or cold.

MAKES 30

175 g/6 oz unsalted butter or
   margarine, plus extra for greasing

225 g/8 oz demerara sugar

1 egg, beaten

4 tbsp milk

1 tsp vanilla essence

½ tsp almond essence

115 g/4 oz hazelnuts

140 g/5 oz plain flour

1½ tsp ground mixed spice

¼ tsp bicarbonate of soda

pinch of salt

300 g/10½ oz porridge oats

150 g/5½ oz sultanas

Oat & Hazelnut Morsels

Try these delicious biscuits with a refreshing cup of mint tea in the afternoon, or give them to hungry children as a snack.

• Preheat the oven to 190°C/375°F/Gas Mark 5. Grease 2 large baking sheets.

• Cream the butter and sugar together in a large mixing bowl. Blend in the egg, milk and vanilla and almond essences until thoroughly combined. Finely chop the hazelnuts.

• In a separate bowl, sift the flour, mixed spice, bicarbonate of soda and salt together. Add to the creamed mixture slowly, stirring constantly. Mix in the oats, sultanas and hazelnuts.

• Put 30 rounded tablespoonfuls of the mixture on to the prepared baking sheets, spaced well apart to allow for spreading. Transfer to the preheated oven and bake for 12–15 minutes, or until the biscuits are golden brown.

• Remove the biscuits from the oven and place on a wire rack to cool before serving.

MAKES 20

225 g/8 oz unsalted butter, plus extra
  for greasing
70 g/2½ oz plain chocolate
125 g/4½ oz plain flour
¾ tsp bicarbonate of soda

¼ tsp baking powder
55 g/2 oz pecan nuts
100 g/3½ oz demerara sugar
½ tsp almond essence
1 egg
1 tsp milk

Pecan Brownies

Pecan nuts are very similar to walnuts, which you can substitute if you prefer.

• Preheat the oven to 180°C/350°F/Gas Mark 4. Grease a large baking dish and line it with baking paper.
• Put the chocolate in a heatproof bowl set over a saucepan of gently simmering water and heat until it is melted. Meanwhile, sift the flour, bicarbonate of soda and baking powder together into a large bowl.
• Finely chop the pecan nuts and set aside. In a separate bowl, cream the butter and sugar together, then mix in the almond essence and the egg. Remove the chocolate from the heat and stir into the butter mixture. Add the flour mixture, milk and chopped nuts to the bowl and stir until well combined.
• Spoon the mixture into the prepared baking dish and smooth it. Transfer to the preheated oven and cook for 30 minutes, or until firm to the touch (it should still be a little soft in the centre). Remove from the oven and leave to cool completely. Cut into 20 squares and serve.

MAKES ABOUT 60

150 g/5½ oz unsalted butter, at
   room temperature, plus extra for
   greasing
150 g/5½ oz caster sugar
115 g/4 oz plain flour

25 g/1 oz ground almonds
pinch of salt
75 g/2¾ oz blanched almonds, lightly
   toasted and finely chopped
finely grated rind of 1 large lemon
4 egg whites

Almond Biscuits

You can toast almonds by dry-frying them in a heavy-based frying pan or by spreading them out on a baking sheet and placing in a preheated oven, 180°C/350°F/Gas Mark 4. They take only a few minutes and it's important to watch them carefully because they burn easily.

• Preheat the oven to 180°C/350°F/Gas Mark 4. Grease 2 baking sheets. Put the butter and sugar into a bowl and beat until light and fluffy. Sift over the flour, ground almonds and salt, tipping in any ground almonds left in the sieve. Use a large metal spoon to fold in the chopped almonds and grated lemon rind.

• In a separate, grease-free bowl, whisk the egg whites until soft peaks form. Fold these into the almond mixture.

• Drop small teaspoonfuls of the biscuit mixture on to the prepared baking sheets, spacing them very well apart to allow for spreading. (You might need to cook in batches.) Bake in a preheated oven for 15–20 minutes until golden brown around the edges. Remove from the oven and transfer to a wire rack to cool completely. Continue baking until all the mixture is used. Store the biscuits in an airtight container for up to 1 week.

MAKES ABOUT 16

115 g/4 oz unsalted butter, softened,
plus extra for greasing

115 g/4 oz light muscovado sugar

85 g/3 oz golden granulated sugar

1 tsp vanilla essence

1 tbsp instant coffee granules,
dissolved in 1 tbsp hot water

1 egg

175 g/6 oz plain flour

½ tsp baking powder

¼ tsp bicarbonate of soda

55 g/2 oz milk chocolate chips

55 g/2 oz shelled walnuts, roughly
chopped

Mocha Walnut Cookies

Muscovado sugar has a tendency to be quite lumpy, so it is a good idea to sieve it before use when baking cakes and biscuits.

• Preheat the oven to 180°C/350°F/Gas Mark 4. Grease 2 large baking sheets with a little butter. Place the butter, muscovado sugar and granulated sugar in a large bowl and thoroughly beat together until light and fluffy. Place the vanilla essence, coffee and egg in a separate large bowl and whisk together.

• Gradually add the coffee mixture to the butter and sugar, beating until fluffy. Sift the flour, baking powder and bicarbonate of soda into the mixture and fold in carefully. Fold in the chocolate chips and walnuts.

• Drop dessertspoonfuls of the mixture onto the prepared baking sheets, spacing well apart to allow room for spreading. Bake in the preheated oven for 10–15 minutes, or until crisp on the outside but still soft inside. Remove from the oven, cool on the baking sheets for 2 minutes, then transfer to wire racks to cool completely.

MAKES 12

115 g/4 oz unsalted butter, plus extra
    for greasing
200 g/7 oz rolled oats
55 g/2 oz hazelnuts, lightly toasted
    and chopped

55 g/2 oz plain flour
85 g/3 oz light muscovado sugar
2 tbsp golden syrup
55 g/2 oz plain chocolate chips

Hazelnut Chocolate Crunch

You can heat the butter,
sugar and syrup in a
microwave oven on
Medium for 2½ minutes
instead of using a
saucepan.

• Preheat the oven to 180°C/350°F/Gas Mark 4. Grease a 23-cm/9-inch shallow, square baking tin. Mix the oats, nuts and flour in a large bowl.

• Place the butter, sugar and syrup in a large saucepan and gently heat until the sugar has dissolved. Pour in the dry ingredients and mix well. Stir in the chocolate chips.

• Turn the mixture into the prepared tin and bake in the preheated oven for 20–25 minutes, or until golden brown and firm to the touch. Using a knife, mark into 12 rectangles and leave to cool in the tin. Cut the hazelnut chocolate crunch bars with a sharp knife before carefully removing them from the tin.

MAKES 24

200 g/7 oz unsalted butter, plus extra
    for greasing
275 g/9½ oz demerara sugar
1 egg
140 g/5 oz plain flour, sieved
1 tsp baking powder

1 tsp bicarbonate of soda
125 g/4½ oz porridge oats
1 tbsp bran
1 tbsp wheatgerm
115 g/4 oz mixed nuts, toasted and
    roughly chopped
200 g/7 oz plain chocolate chips

115 g/4 oz raisins and sultanas
175 g/6 oz plain chocolate, roughly
    chopped

Nutty Drizzles

Porridge oats are also
sometimes labelled
oatflakes or rolled oats
(but not oatmeal).

• Preheat the oven to 180°C/350°F/Gas Mark 4. Grease 2 large baking sheets. In a large bowl, cream the butter, sugar and egg together. Add the flour, baking powder, bicarbonate of soda, oats, bran and wheatgerm and mix together until well combined. Finally, stir in the nuts, chocolate chips and dried fruit.

• Put 24 rounded tablespoonfuls of the mixture onto the prepared baking sheets, spaced well apart to allow for spreading. Transfer to the preheated oven and bake for 12 minutes, or until the biscuits are golden brown.

• Remove the biscuits from the oven, then transfer to a wire rack and leave to cool. Meanwhile, heat the chocolate pieces in a heatproof bowl set over a saucepan of gently simmering water until melted. Stir the chocolate, then leave to cool slightly. Use a spoon to drizzle the chocolate in waves over the biscuits, or spoon it into a piping bag and pipe zigzag lines over the biscuits. When the chocolate has set, store the biscuits in an airtight container in the refrigerator until ready to serve.

Nutritionists recommend that we eat five portions of fruit and vegetables a day, but this is not always practical and can prove to be quite a problem, especially if you have fussy eaters in your household. The scrumptious nibbles in this chapter include apricots, figs, cherries, dates, currants, raisins, sultanas and bananas, combined with a mouth-watering range of other ingredients as varied as nuts, seeds, oats, honey, spices, chocolate and fruit juice. They are sure to be a runaway success with every member of the family – and, of course, there is no need for you to tell anyone that these tasty snacks are actually quite healthy, too.

Fruit bars are ideal for the school lunch box and can also provide a kick-start to the day for busy adults who have no time for breakfast. They make a great pick-me-up whenever your energy is flagging and are the perfect after-school snack for kids.

FRUITFUL ENDEAVOURS

From Apricot Flapjacks to Caribbean Cookies, the recipes in this chapter are easy to follow, quick and economical, so there is no excuse for not having a ready supply of tasty treats to hand. Furthermore, many of the ingredients for these cookies and bars are storecupboard staples, such as honey, porridge oats and dried fruit. It is easy to substitute one kind of dried fruit for another – dates instead of figs or sultanas instead of raisins – so you can customize your baking to your resources and, more importantly, to your family's tastes. Do keep an eye on the 'use-by' dates on the packets to ensure that your biscuits have the best and freshest flavour.

MAKES 10

sunflower oil, for oiling

175 g/6 oz polyunsaturated spread

85 g/3 oz demerara sugar

clear honey

140 g/5 oz ready-to-eat dried apricots,
    chopped

2 tsp sesame seeds

225 g/8 oz porridge oats

Apricot Flapjacks

Ready-to-eat dried apricots are ideal for this recipe, because they do not need soaking. You could use dried figs, dates or muscatel raisins for a change of flavour.

• Preheat the oven to 180°C/350°F/Gas Mark 4. Very lightly oil a 26 x 17-cm/10½ x 6½-inch shallow cake tin.
• Put the spread, sugar and honey into a small saucepan over a low heat and heat until the ingredients have melted together – do not allow the mixture to boil. When the ingredients are warm and well combined, stir in the apricots, sesame seeds and oats.
• Spoon the mixture into the prepared tin and lightly level with the back of a spoon. Cook in the preheated oven for 20–25 minutes or until golden brown. Remove from the oven, cut into 10 bars and leave to cool completely before removing from the cake tin. Store the flapjacks in an airtight container and consume within 2–3 days.

MAKES 20

225 g/8 oz unsalted butter or
    margarine, plus extra for greasing

75 g/2¾ oz dried figs

115 g/4 oz clear honey

4 tbsp demerara sugar

2 eggs, beaten

pinch of salt

1 tsp mixed spice

1 tsp bicarbonate of soda

½ tsp vanilla essence

2 tbsp dried dates, finely chopped

225 g/8 oz plain flour

175 g/6 oz porridge oats

40 g/1½ oz walnuts, finely chopped

dried fig pieces, to decorate (optional)

Fig & Walnut Biscuits

When making creamed
mixtures, remove the
butter from the refrigerator
about 30 minutes before
you need to use it to let it
come to room temperature
and soften slightly.

- Preheat the oven to 180°C/350°F/Gas Mark 4. Grease 2 large baking sheets.
- Finely chop the figs. Mix the butter, honey, figs and sugar together in a large bowl. Beat the eggs into the mixture and thoroughly mix.
- In a separate bowl, combine the salt, mixed spice, bicarbonate of soda, vanilla essence and dates. Gradually stir them into the creamed mixture. Sift the flour into the mixture and stir well. Finally, mix in the oats and walnuts.
- Drop 20 rounded tablespoonfuls of the mixture on to the prepared baking sheets, spaced well apart to allow for spreading. Decorate with fig pieces, if using. Bake in the preheated oven for 10–15 minutes, or until the biscuits are golden brown.
- Remove the biscuits from the oven, transfer to a wire rack and leave to cool before serving.

MAKES ABOUT 14

55 g/2 oz unsalted butter

40 g/1½ oz demerara sugar

1 tbsp golden syrup

55 g/2 oz plain flour, sieved

25 g/1 oz angelica, roughly chopped

25 g/1 oz glacé cherries, roughly
chopped

55 g/2 oz flaked almonds, roughly
chopped

55 g/2 oz glacé pineapple, roughly
chopped

1 tsp lemon juice

115 g/4 oz plain chocolate, melted and
cooled

Pineapple & Cherry Florentines

If you have difficulty removing the florentines from the baking sheet, return them to the oven for 2 minutes, then lift off and cool on a wire rack.

• Preheat the oven to 180°C/350°F/Gas Mark 4. Line 1 or 2 large baking sheets with non-stick baking paper. Place the butter, sugar and syrup in a saucepan and heat gently until melted, then stir in the flour, angelica, cherries, almonds, pineapple and lemon juice.

• Place walnut-sized mounds of the mixture spaced well apart on the prepared baking sheets and flatten gently with a fork. Bake in the preheated oven for 8–10 minutes, or until golden. Use a palette knife to neaten the ragged edges. Leave to cool for 1 minute, then transfer to a wire rack to cool completely.

• Spread the melted chocolate over the base of each florentine, placing the biscuits, chocolate side up, on a wire rack. Use a fork to mark the chocolate with wavy lines. Leave until set.

MAKES 36

125 g/4½ oz unsalted butter or
    margarine, plus extra for greasing
175 g/6 oz ready-to-eat dried apricots
85 g/3 oz dried dates

140 g/5 oz plain flour
75 g/2¾ oz porridge oats
90 g/3¼ oz wheat flakes
½ tsp bicarbonate of soda
pinch of salt

140 g/5 oz soft brown sugar, plus
    extra for dusting
2 eggs
1 tsp almond essence

Fruit Morsels

You can chop dried fruit with a heavy-bladed kitchen knife or snip it into pieces with a pair of strong kitchen scissors – whichever is easier.

• Preheat the oven to 190°C/375°F/Gas Mark 5. Grease 2 large baking sheets with butter. Chop the dried apricots and dates. Sift the flour into a large bowl and mix in the oats, wheat flakes, bicarbonate of soda and salt.
• In a separate bowl, blend the sugar and butter together. Beat in the eggs until the mixture is light and fluffy. Gradually add the flour mixture, stirring. Blend in the almond essence and fruit. Mix well.
• Drop 36 teaspoonfuls of the mixture on to the prepared baking sheets, spaced very well apart to allow for spreading. Dust with sugar. Bake for 10 minutes, or until golden brown.
• Remove the biscuits from the oven, place on a wire rack and leave them to cool before serving.

MAKES 24

unsalted butter, for greasing

25 g/1 oz mashed banana

1 tbsp pineapple juice

1 tbsp orange juice

4 tbsp groundnut oil

1 egg

1 tbsp milk

140 g/5 oz plain flour

¼ tsp bicarbonate of soda

75 g/2¾ oz desiccated coconut

demerara sugar, for sprinkling

Caribbean Cookies

If you prefer, substitute grated fresh coconut for the desiccated. You could also use finely chopped, very ripe mango instead of the mashed banana.

• Preheat the oven to 180°C/350°F/Gas Mark 4. Grease a large baking sheet.
• In a large bowl, cream the banana, fruit juices, oil, egg and milk together. Transfer the mixture to a food mixer.
• With the machine running, sift in the flour and bicarbonate of soda, beating constantly. Add the desiccated coconut and mix well.
• Drop rounded teaspoonfuls on to the prepared baking sheet, spaced well apart to allow for spreading. Sprinkle with the demerara sugar, then transfer to the preheated oven and bake for about 10 minutes, or until the cookies are golden brown.
• Remove the cookies from the oven and transfer to a wire rack to cool before serving.

MAKES 9

115 g/4 oz unsalted butter, plus extra
    for greasing
2 tbsp clear honey
1 egg, beaten
85 g/3 oz ground almonds

115 g/4 oz ready-to-eat dried apricots,
    finely chopped
55 g/2 oz dried cherries
55 g/2 oz toasted hazelnuts
25 g/1 oz sesame seeds
85 g/3 oz jumbo oats

Fruit & Nut Squares

The easiest way to smooth the surface of the mixture is with the back of a slightly damp tablespoon or a damp palette knife. Smoothing the surface ensures that the mixture bakes through and is an even golden brown.

• Preheat the oven to 180°C/350°F/Gas Mark 4. Lightly grease an 18-cm/7-inch shallow, square cake tin with butter. Beat the remaining butter with the honey in a bowl until creamy, then beat in the egg with the almonds.

• Add the remaining ingredients and mix together well. Press into the prepared tin, ensuring that the mixture is firmly packed. Smooth the top.

• Transfer to the preheated oven and bake for 20–25 minutes, or until firm to the touch and golden brown.

• Remove from the oven and leave to stand for 10 minutes before marking into squares. Leave until cold before removing from the tin. Cut into squares and store in an airtight container.

MAKES 30

175 g/6 oz unsalted butter or
  margarine, plus extra for greasing
200 g/7 oz soft brown sugar
2 eggs
350 g/12 oz plain flour

pinch of salt
2 tsp baking powder
2 tbsp milk
1 tsp almond essence
150 g/5½ oz chopped walnuts
75 g/2¾ oz raisins

75 g/2¾ oz sultanas
100 g/3½ oz maraschino cherries
200 g/7 oz wheat flakes, crushed
15 maraschino cherries, halved,
  to decorate

Cherry & Walnut Biscuits

The slightly bitter flavour of maraschino cherries gives these biscuits an intriguing flavour. However, you could use sweet cherries if you prefer.

• Preheat the oven to 190°C/375°F/Gas Mark 5. Grease 1 or 2 large baking sheets.
• Cream the butter and sugar in a large mixing bowl until the mixture is light and fluffy. Beat in the eggs.
• Gradually sift the flour, salt and baking powder into the creamed mixture. Add the milk and almond essence and thoroughly mix. Stir in the walnuts, dried fruit and maraschino cherries.
• Form the dough into 30 balls (about 1 rounded tablespoon each) and roll in the crushed wheat flakes. Place the dough balls on the prepared baking sheet, spaced about 2.5 cm/1 inch apart. Place half a maraschino cherry on the top of each dough ball. Transfer to the preheated oven and cook for 10 minutes, or until the biscuits are light brown. Transfer from the oven to a wire rack and leave to cool completely before serving.

MAKES 16

200 g/7 oz unsalted butter, plus extra
    for greasing
200 g/7 oz demerara sugar

2 tbsp golden syrup
275 g/9½ oz porridge oats
100 g/3½ oz desiccated coconut
75 g/2¾ oz glacé cherries, chopped

Coconut Flapjacks

Store flapjacks in an airtight container and eat within 1 week. They can also be frozen for up to 1 month.

• Preheat the oven to 160°C/325°F/Gas Mark 3. Grease a 30 x 23-cm/12 x 9-inch baking tray.

• Put the butter, sugar and syrup in a large saucepan and set over a low heat until just melted. Stir in the oats, coconut and cherries and mix until evenly combined.

• Evenly spread the mixture onto the baking tray and press down with the back of a spatula or palette knife to make a smooth surface.

• Bake in the preheated oven for 30 minutes. Remove from the oven and leave to cool on the baking tray for 10 minutes. Using a sharp knife, cut the flapjack into rectangles. Carefully transfer the pieces of flapjack to a wire rack and leave to cool completely.

MAKES 16

225 g/8 oz plain flour

1 tsp baking powder

100 g/3½ oz caster sugar

85 g/3 oz soft brown sugar

225 g/8 oz unsalted butter

150 g/5½ oz porridge oats

225 g/8 oz strawberry jam

100 g/3½ oz plain chocolate chips

25 g/1 oz almonds, chopped

Strawberry & Chocolate Slices

Other flavours of jam also go well with chocolate. Raspberry is a classic partner, but you may want to sieve out any pips before spreading it over the cooked base.

• Preheat the oven to 190°C/375°F/Gas Mark 5. Line a 30 x 20-cm/12 x 8-inch deep-sided Swiss roll tin with baking paper. Sift the flour and baking powder into a large bowl.

• Add the caster sugar and brown sugar to the flour and mix well. Add the butter and rub in until the mixture resembles breadcrumbs. Stir in the oats.

• Press three-quarters of the mixture into the base of the prepared cake tin. Bake in the preheated oven for 10 minutes.

• Spread the jam over the cooked base, then sprinkle over the chocolate chips. Mix the remaining flour mixture with the almonds. Evenly sprinkle the mixture over the chocolate chips and press down gently.

• Return to the oven and bake for a further 20–25 minutes until golden brown. Remove from the oven, leave to cool in the tin, then cut into slices.

All homemade cookies and bars are special, but the ones in this chapter have that little something extra, whether charming, dainty Vanilla Hearts – perfect for a wedding anniversary morning tea tray – or Lavender Cookies – the epitome of elegance for a sunny tea party on the lawn.

Lots of occasions call for a special treat, and in this chapter you are sure to find a delicious but easy recipe for just the right tempting little snack, whether for a Christmas treat, a tea tray to welcome new neighbours, a school summer fair or just to spoil the family. Homemade biscuits also make delightful presents, especially if you pack them in an attractive box or wrap them in cellophane tied with a colourful ribbon. You could even give a delicate cup and saucer packed with special biscuits.

SOMETHING SPECIAL

Many of the biscuits in this chapter are also wonderful accompaniments to creamy desserts and ice cream, adding a subtle but impressive flourish to any formal dinner party. And, of course, Amaretti, those crunchy, almond-flavoured, moreish morsels from Italy, are traditionally served to guests with a glass of chilled white wine, whatever the time of day.

Allow just a little more time for the recipes in this chapter, mainly because most of the biscuits have extra decoration, so you will need time for them to cool and for icing or melted chocolate to set. However, you are sure to find that this little extra effort is well worth it when you see how fast the biscuits disappear from the plate.

MAKES 12

125 g/4½ oz unsalted butter, softened

75 g/2¾ oz golden icing sugar

125 g/4½ oz plain flour

40 g/1½ oz cocoa powder

½ tsp ground cinnamon

FILLING

125 g/4½ oz plain chocolate, broken
   into pieces

50 ml/2 fl oz double cream

Cookies & Cream Sandwiches

Do not sandwich the biscuits together too long before serving, otherwise they will go soft. Store unsandwiched biscuits in an airtight container for up to 3 days.

• Preheat the oven to 160°C/325°F/Gas Mark 3. Line a baking sheet with non-stick baking paper. Place the butter and sugar in a large bowl and beat together until light and fluffy. Sift the flour, cocoa powder and ground cinnamon into the bowl and mix until a smooth dough forms.

• Place the dough between 2 sheets of non-stick baking paper and roll out to 3 mm/⅛ inch thick. Stamp out 6-cm/2½-inch rounds and place on the prepared baking sheet. Bake in the preheated oven for 15 minutes, or until firm to the touch. Leave to cool for 2 minutes, then transfer to wire racks to cool completely.

• To make the filling, place the chocolate and cream in a saucepan and gently heat until the chocolate has melted. Stir until smooth. Leave to cool, then leave to chill in the refrigerator for 2 hours, or until firm. Sandwich the biscuits together in pairs with a spoonful of chocolate cream and serve.

MAKES ABOUT 40
150 g/5½ oz blanched almonds
150 g/5½ oz caster sugar
1 large egg white
icing sugar, for dusting

Amaretti

To intensify the almond flavour, add a drop or two of almond essence with the egg white. This is the secret of the popular Amaretti di Saronno. You could also wrap individual biscuits in colourful tissue paper if you are planning to give them as a gift.

• Preheat the oven to 120°C/250°F/Gas Mark ½. Use a pestle and mortar to crush the almonds with the caster sugar, or finely chop the almonds and then combine with the sugar in a bowl.
• Lightly beat the egg white, then stir it into the almond mixture to form a firm dough. Line 2 large baking sheets with baking paper and place walnut-sized portions of the dough on them, spaced well apart to allow for spreading. Dust with icing sugar. Bake in the preheated oven for 30 minutes. Remove from the oven and transfer to wire racks to cool completely.

MAKES 40

225 g/8 oz unsalted butter, softened,
    plus extra for greasing
55 g/2 oz golden caster sugar
225 g/8 oz plain flour

115 g/4 oz cornflour
1 tsp ground cinnamon
55 g/2 oz sieved icing sugar,
    to decorate

Mexican Pastelitos

These biscuits are traditionally made in this small size, but you could make larger biscuits, if you prefer.

• Preheat the oven to 160°C/325°F/Gas Mark 3. Grease 2 baking sheets. Place the butter and caster sugar in a bowl and beat until light and fluffy. Sift the flour, cornflour and cinnamon into a separate bowl, then gradually work them into the creamed mixture with a wooden spoon. When well mixed, knead until smooth.

• Take 1 teaspoon at a time of the mixture and roll into a ball. Place the little balls on the prepared baking sheets. Bake in the preheated oven for 30–40 minutes, or until pale golden.

• Place the icing sugar in a shallow dish and toss the pastelitos in it while they are still warm. Leave to cool on wire racks.

MAKES ABOUT 30

115 g/4 oz unsalted butter, softened,
    plus extra for greasing
55 g/2 oz golden icing sugar, sieved

125 g/4½ oz plain flour
1 tbsp cocoa powder
100 g/3½ oz plain chocolate, melted
    and cooled

Chocolate Viennese Fingers

Sprinkle some chopped
nuts on to the chocolate-
coated ends of these
biscuits while the chocolate
is still soft, if you like.

• Preheat the oven to 180°C/350°F/Gas Mark 4. Grease 2 large baking sheets. Beat the butter and sugar together until light and fluffy. Sift the flour and cocoa powder into the bowl and work the mixture until it is a smooth, piping consistency.

• Spoon into a large piping bag fitted with a 2.5-cm/1-inch star nozzle. Pipe 6-cm/2½-inch lengths of the mixture on to the prepared baking sheets, spacing them well apart to allow for spreading. Bake in the preheated oven for 15 minutes, or until firm.

• Remove from the oven and leave to cool on the baking sheets for 2 minutes, then transfer to a wire rack to cool completely. Dip the ends of the biscuits into the melted chocolate and leave to set before serving.

MAKES 12

150 g/5½ oz unsalted butter, cut
    into small pieces, plus extra for
    greasing
225 g/8 oz plain flour, plus extra for
    dusting

125 g/4½ oz caster sugar, plus extra
    for dusting
1 tsp vanilla essence

Vanilla Hearts

Place a fresh vanilla pod in your caster sugar and keep it in a storage jar for several weeks to give the sugar a delicious vanilla flavour.

• Preheat the oven to 180°C/350°F/Gas Mark 4. Lightly grease a large baking sheet. Sift the flour into a large bowl. Add the butter and rub in with your fingertips until the mixture resembles fine breadcrumbs. Stir in the caster sugar and vanilla essence and mix together to form a firm dough.

• Roll out the dough on a lightly floured work surface to a thickness of 2.5 cm/1 inch. Stamp out 12 hearts with a heart-shaped biscuit cutter measuring about 5 cm/2 inches across and 2.5 cm/1 inch deep. Arrange the hearts on the prepared baking sheet.

• Transfer to the preheated oven and bake for 15–20 minutes, or until the hearts are a light golden colour. Transfer the vanilla hearts to a wire rack and leave to cool completely. Dust them with caster sugar just before serving.

MAKES 12

55 g/2 oz unsalted butter, plus extra
    for greasing

55 g/2 oz raisins

2 tbsp brandy

115 g/4 oz plain chocolate, broken into
    pieces

115 g/4 oz milk chocolate, broken into
    pieces

2 tbsp golden syrup

175 g/6 oz digestive biscuits, roughly
    broken

55 g/2 oz flaked almonds, lightly
    toasted

25 g/1 oz glacé cherries, chopped

TOPPING

100 g/3½ oz plain chocolate, broken
    into pieces

20 g/¾ oz butter

Tiffin

For a decorative effect, use a fork to mark light wavy lines over the chocolate topping before leaving it to set in the refrigerator.

• Grease and line the base of an 18-cm/7-inch shallow, square cake tin. Place the raisins and brandy in a bowl and leave to soak for about 30 minutes. Put the chocolate, butter and syrup in a saucepan and heat gently until melted.

• Stir in the digestive biscuits, almonds, cherries, raisins and brandy. Turn into the prepared tin and leave to cool. Cover and leave to chill in the refrigerator for 1 hour.

• To make the topping, place the chocolate and butter in a small heatproof bowl and set over a saucepan of gently simmering water until melted. Stir and pour over the biscuit base. Leave to chill in the refrigerator for 8 hours or overnight. Cut into bars or squares to serve.

MAKES 24

175 g/6 oz unsalted butter,
   plus extra for greasing
55 g/2 oz eating apple,
   cored and cooked
50 g/1¾ oz soft brown sugar
5 tbsp molasses
1 egg white

1 tsp almond essence
200 g/7 oz plain flour
¼ tsp bicarbonate of soda
¼ tsp baking powder
pinch of salt
½ tsp mixed spice
½ tsp ground ginger

Gingerbread Squares

Mixed spice is exactly what it says on the label but you could substitute your own combination of spices, such as ground cinnamon, freshly grated nutmeg or mace and ground cloves.

• Preheat the oven to 180°C/350°F/Gas Mark 4. Grease a large cake tin and line it with baking paper. Chop the apple and set aside. Put the butter, sugar, molasses, egg white and almond essence in a food processor and process until the mixture is smooth.

• Sift the flour, bicarbonate of soda, baking powder, salt, mixed spice and ginger together in another bowl. Add to the creamed mixture and beat together well until combined. Stir the apple into the mixture, then pour the mixture into the prepared cake tin.

• Transfer to the preheated oven and bake for 10 minutes, or until golden brown. Remove from the oven and cut into 24 pieces. Transfer the gingerbread to a wire rack and leave to cool completely before serving.

MAKES 20

140 g/5 oz unsalted butter

115 g/4 oz caster sugar

1 egg yolk

115 g/4 oz ground almonds

175 g/6 oz plain flour

55 g/2 oz plain chocolate,
   broken into pieces

2 tbsp icing sugar

2 tbsp cocoa powder

Ladies' Kisses

Place the dough balls well apart from each other on the baking sheets because they will spread out during cooking. You may need to cook the biscuits in batches.

• Line 3 baking sheets with baking paper or use non-stick sheets. Beat the butter and caster sugar together in a bowl until pale and fluffy. Beat in the egg yolk, then the almonds and flour. Continue beating until well mixed. Shape the dough into a ball, wrap in clingfilm and leave to chill in the refrigerator for 1½–2 hours.

• Preheat the oven to 160°C/325°F/Gas Mark 3. Unwrap the dough, break off walnut-sized pieces and roll them into balls between the palms of your hands. Place the dough balls on the prepared baking sheets, spaced well apart to allow for spreading. Bake in the preheated oven for 20–25 minutes, or until golden brown. Remove from the oven and carefully transfer the biscuits, still on the baking paper if using, to wire racks to cool.

• Place the plain chocolate in a small heatproof bowl set over a saucepan of gently simmering water, and stir constantly until melted. Remove the bowl from the heat. Remove the biscuits from the baking paper, if using, and spread the melted chocolate over the bases. Sandwich them together in pairs and return to the wire racks to cool and set. Dust with a mixture of sifted icing sugar and cocoa powder and serve.

MAKES 12

115 g/4 oz unsalted butter,
    softened, plus extra for greasing
55 g/2 oz golden caster sugar,
    plus extra for dusting

1 tsp chopped lavender leaves
finely grated rind of 1 lemon
175 g/6 oz plain flour

Lavender Cookies

If you do not have a food processor, you can mix the dough by hand. Knead it into a ball before rolling the dough out.

• Preheat the oven to 150°C/300°F/Gas Mark 2, then grease a large baking sheet. Place the caster sugar and lavender leaves in a food processor. Process until the lavender is very finely chopped, then add the butter and lemon rind and process until light and fluffy. Transfer to a large bowl. Sift in the flour and beat until the mixture forms a stiff dough.

• Place the dough on a sheet of baking paper and place another sheet on top. Gently press down with a rolling pin and roll out to 3–5 mm/⅛–¼ inch thick. Remove the top sheet of paper and stamp out circles from the dough using a 7-cm/2¾-inch round biscuit cutter. Re-knead and re-roll the trimmings and stamp out more biscuits.

• Using a palette knife, carefully transfer the biscuits to the prepared baking sheet. Prick them with a fork and bake in the preheated oven for 12 minutes, or until pale brown. Remove from the oven, cool on the baking sheet for 2 minutes, then transfer to a wire rack to cool completely.

Index

Index

Index